The
BUMPER
book of
DONKEYS

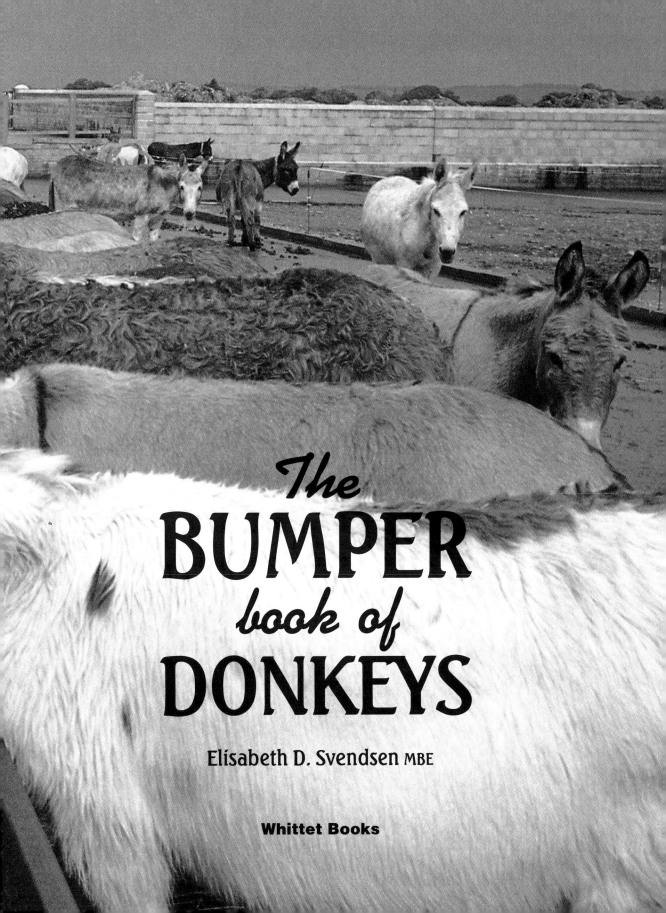

The BUMPER book of DONKEYS

Elisabeth D. Svendsen MBE

Whittet Books

Many thanks to all the contributors to the book:
The Late Neil Harvey, John Axe, Paddy Barrett, Heather Brown, Julie Policutt-Courtney, Tony Downs, Bert Duncan, John Fry, Deirdre Golden, Sydney Judge, Diana Murray, Malcolm Salter, Gill Pudenz, Sue Walker, June Evers, Paul Svendsen, Peter Venus, Mr & Mrs Barwick, Nicola and Andrew Combes, Mr & Mrs Brooker, Mr & Mrs Freeman Dunn, Mr & Mrs Wright, Susan Webster, Mrs Lightfoot, Sheila Rabjohns, Mr & Mrs Paine, Betty Matthews, Stan Bellamy, Julie Martin, Bill Cooper, Mary Hubbard & Ann Heney, Pat Downey, Mo Flenley, Sylvia Horne, Fred Lang, Stan Dowse, Mrs Dorothy Ward, Miss U. Westell, Donkey Breed Society Juniors, Kylie Elliott, Dawn Hart, Sharleen Walker, Sue Brennan, Robert Camac, Geoffrey Ford, Mrs V. Kearney, The Late Mrs Joan Couzens, Ellen Summers, Felicia M. Carran, Margaret Riley, John Howard Bennett, Vanadia Sandon-Humphries, Peggy Judge, Sally-Anne Hardie, Sue Ann Weaver.

Photographs and illustrations appear by kind permission of the following (listed by order in which their first picture appears in the book):
Mo Flenley, p. 1, p. 128; June Evers, pp. 2/3, p. 15, p. 45, p. 46, p. 47, p. 48, p. 62, p. 67, p. 72, p. 116, p. 120, p. 126, p. 135, p. 138, p. 143; *Woman's Own*, p. 9; Dorothy Morris, p. 13, p. 25; *Your Horse*, p. 22, p. 85; Henry Phillips, p. 27, p. 121; Robert Camac, p. 30; Julie Courtney, p. 35; *Pulman's Weekly News*, p. 40; *South Wales Evening Post*, p. 43; Karl-Heinz Raach, p. 39; *Daily Star*, p. 51; Sophie Thurnham, p. 53; Len Shepherd, p. 59; Michael Viney, p. 65; Rita Barton, p. 70, p. 73, p. 78, p. 119, p. 154, p. 175; Elizabeth Peters, p. 76; Mr & Mrs Venus, p. 77; Mr & Mrs Barwick, p. 79; *East Anglian Daily Times*, p. 86, Mr H J Bye, p. 88; Mr & Mrs Brooker (2), p. 90; *Western Mail*, p. 93; Mrs Freeman Dunn, p. 95; *Greenock Telegraph*, p. 96; Susan Webster, p. 99; Mrs Preston, p. 101; Joan Lightfoot, p. 102; Nicholas Toyne, p. 106, 118; *Ormskirk Advertiser*, p. 111, *Exeter Express and Echo*, p. 113; Elspeth Cargill, pp. 10/11, p. 130; Dorothy Ward, p. 139, Paul Svendsen, p. 163

Extracts from newspapers and magazines are reprinted by kind permission of the following:
Newport News, Pulman's Weekly News, Sporting Life, Westmoreland Gazette, Maldon and Burnham Standard, Derby Evening Telegraph, Ashbourne News Telegraph, Western Mail, Cardiff, *Western Morning News, Irish Times/Agence France Presse, Ormskirk Advertiser, Greenock Telegraph, Belfast Newsletter, The Times, Glasgow Herald, Irish Times, South Wales Evening Post, Daily Telegraph, Exeter Express and Echo, The Brayer, Midwest Equine Market* and *Horseman's Guide*.

(Half title page illustration) 'I thought the book was really funny.'

(Title page illustration) Some happy residents at the Donkey Sanctuary.

Dedication

To all the staff at the Donkey Sanctuary, without whose help the donkey work could not go on and to those many loyal supporters who keep the donkeys in such comfort by their donations.

First published 1991
© 1991 by Elisabeth D. Svendsen
Whittet Books Ltd, 18 Anley Road, London W14 0BY
Design by Richard Kelly

The Donkey Sanctuary is at Sidmouth, Devon.
The telephone number is 0395 578222

British Library Cataloguing in Publication Data
Svendsen, Elizabeth D.
The bumper book of donkeys.
1. Donkeys
I. Title
636.18

ISBN 0-905483-89-8

Typeset by Litho Link Ltd., Welshpool, Powys.
Printed and bound in Hong Kong
by South China Printing Co.

Contents

Foreword

I love many things in life, but there is no doubt in my mind that the donkey must take priority. Living a life with donkeys has opened the door to experiences I would previously never have thought possible. Some have been sad, some hilarious, but all have been interesting and all have given me a purpose for living.

I have just reached my 60th birthday, and in a way this book celebrates the event. I really thought the date was one of the best kept secrets of the year but I just couldn't have been more mistaken!

I was busy working in my aviary, where I have nearly a hundred rescued birds, when my son Paul arrived on that particular morning, January 23rd, at half past seven, with a silly grin on his face and a video camera in his hand.

'Happy birthday, Mum,' he said, beaming all over his face, and all 6ft 4in of him towering over me, as he put his arm round me and gave me a birthday kiss.

'Oh thank you, darling,' I replied, 'but what are you doing here so early?'

'Oh,' said Paul nonchalantly, 'I just thought I'd see you across to the office on your birthday morning.'

I suppose at this stage I should have guessed that the cat was out of the bag, but even then I could never have anticipated the treats in store for me that day. It started with the balloons and the WELCOME SIXTY at the office door, and from there on, with the zimmer frame, a wheelchair and a very enlarged facsimile of my old-age pension book and a senior citizen's rail card, the day was to be one long hilarious party. It included the most marvellous gift-giving ceremony from the staff, at which my emotions rather overcame me yet again, and culminated in Sam and Dobby, the donkeys, arriving dressed up like show horses pulling a beautifully decorated cart to take me to the Slade Centre where a large group of handicapped children were waiting to sing 'Happy Birthday' to me and to cut a big cake. All the staff turned up as well and it really was a most memorable day.

Reaching sixty has its advantages; not only the old age pension but now reduced rates on rail travel. Recently, travelling through Bristol, I stopped at the service station and was delighted to see that I could get a pot of tea and help myself to a bun from a specially prepared basket of goodies just for OAPs 'at only 90 pence'!

I appreciate how very lucky I am having such a wonderful job which totally absorbs the whole of my life and which allows me the immense satisfaction of being able to help both people and animals who are in need and who have no one else to turn to. I meet many elderly and lonely people in my life and I do feel that as we grow older we should make every effort to take a companion if life has been cruel enough to separate us from our chosen loved ones at an early age. I see many elderly lonely people living within a short distance of others in similar situations and it occurs to me that perhaps two older women or perhaps two older men (or perhaps one of each?) could strike up a friendship which would be of great benefit to both partners. Not only would there be the benefit of sharing the expenses of today's modern living, which are very high, but it would give each person a reason for living, someone to turn to, someone to help and be helped by should they need assistance at any time.

If it's impossible to find someone to live with, then I don't think there's any doubt in my mind that the answer for older people is to have an animal companion of some sort. Very often, the companionship of a small dog or a cat can make all the difference to an empty, futile-seeming life. Animals can give an immense amount to their owners and in return the owner can give a full and happy life to a creature very often in need of help. And I don't just mean dogs and cats. Many elderly people would be incapable of taking even a small dog out for a walk; smaller species might be the answer; they can be given a real sense of freedom with the minimum amount of effort on the part of the owner. How often do you see hamsters in pet shops stuck in tiny cages with almost nothing to do and nothing to help pass their days? Larger runs with 'toys' in them can give these creatures a much better life; I kept hamsters when I was younger and they gave me innumerable hours of pleasure watching them in the special habitat I had designed for them, and I know that they lived a happy and full life without terrible boredom which must overcome most small animals in captivity.

This book is, however, mainly about donkeys and is designed for all ages! It contains ideas on fund-raising (which can be used for any other charity), crafts incorporating donkeys, a children's corner and some of the goings-on behind the scenes at the Donkey Sanctuary; stories of donkeys that have happily been placed in homes and some of the more humorous situations I've found myself in abroad; also numerous items of interest from press cuttings and poems, photographs and letters, all, of course, to do with my favourite species – the DONKEY. None of this could have been done without the superb support, not only from my staff, but from donkey lovers and supporters everywhere.

I hope you enjoy it!

Elisabeth D. Svendsen, M.B.E.

BEHIND THE SCENES AT THE DONKEY SANCTUARY

Donkey visitors.

Filming

We are always being asked by the media to take part in films and to pose for photographs; film crews from as far afield as France and Germany have come to visit and, of course, numerous ones from the UK. They all seem to have one great desire, and that is to film me surrounded by as many donkeys as possible. While this sounds easy, and indeed should be easy since all the donkeys are extremely affectionate and loving, there are always problems of toes being trodden on and that cheeky donkey who just wants an extra little nip of one's backside at the wrong moment. All, of course, in the name of love and affection. I usually have a pocketful of polo mints and a few carrots to encourage the donkeys, as television crews can take an incredibly long time in getting the actual shot 'in the can'. If I'm also asked to speak on film then this causes even more problems. We have to stop if a dog barks, a donkey brays, a car starts in the area, or if someone simply shouts across, 'Hello, Mrs S, can I see you a moment?'

One day we were on about the sixth 'take' of a particularly difficult shot in the field for a programme that was to go out on the BBC and I kept trying to warn the crew that the sea mist was rolling in. To those of you who aren't used to our area, it's almost impossible to describe how one moment everything is marvellously sunny and clear and the next you are enclosed in a thick rolling mist. This is exactly what happened on that particular day. It didn't affect me too much, I was already surrounded by donkeys and we had all got used to standing around patiently waiting, but it did affect the cameraman, who had decided that he would climb up a ladder in order to get this very special shot. I must have faded from view at the same time as a group of donkeys decided that the ladder was more interesting than I was and the first I knew of the problem was when I heard a muffled shriek and ran down to find the cameraman picking himself up and saying rather uncomplimentary things about the donkeys. Apparently, two inquisitive donkeys had managed to approach from each side of the ladder and had completely concertinaed it. The poor cameraman got a much closer shot of the donkeys than he would probably have liked.

Waiting to be filmed.

12

Creatures Great and Small

I suppose it's quite natural that, loving donkeys as I do, I also have a great affection for other animals; some years ago, as I walked through our woodland area, I thought how nice it would be if a few little pigs were allowed to wander free and live a natural life in our unused woodland. Julie Courtney, our Assistant Administrator, had long been fond of pigs in general and 'Snowdrop' her beautiful Middlewhite pig in particular. Snowdrop was almost one of the family and an extremely affectionate pig. When I approached Julie to ask if she knew where I could find a nice pig or two, she suggested I rang Mrs Mills at Gilhouse Farm. This I did, and was invited down to have a look at two litters, one of Middlewhites and one of Berkshire Gilts. My life-long friend June and I set off down to Crediton and were absolutely entranced with both mothers and litters, and promptly made an offer for a piglet from each litter. We waited until they were three months old and then on November 5th, 1984, we had the great pleasure of receiving our first two 'wiggies' as they became known!

Charlotte had a very impressive name, Gilhouse Royal Lustre 53, whilst Victoria was Gilhouse Fair Lady 30. They soon answered to their names of Charlotte and Victoria and took over one of the small stables in the Sanctuary until they were big enough to move down to their full-time quarters in the woods. Pigs are certainly very affectionate and both June and I spent a lot of time with them in the evenings, thoroughly enjoying their antics; they would do almost anything for a piece of apple or a biscuit. We decided we would register them, as they were both pedigree pigs, but I'm afraid on finding that we would have to pierce their ears to put tags on we decided against this.

Both Charlotte and Victoria grew bigger and bigger and fatter and fatter, and on receipt of a phone call from Mrs Mills suggesting that it was time they perhaps met the boar, off they went the following May with all the necessary paperwork for what could be classed as their marriage ceremony! Safely back with us, we awaited the happy events with some trepidation, as we were so fond of them both we would have hated anything to go wrong for them. We really had missed them during the three weeks they were with the boar. After innumerable visits, on the evening of September 5th I found Victoria lying on her side and in no time at all, and with no trouble, twelve little piglets were crawling around her, making funny little snorting noises and looking absolutely adorable. Our vet came round to make sure that all was well, and

Bill Loosemore with the 'wiggies'.

was most concerned to see me in the box holding Victoria's head; he was very hesitant about entering the stable, as apparently pigs can get vicious during farrowing. He said he knew of many vets who had nasty injuries which had been caused at this time. Of course he didn't know Victoria as well as we did and she seemed to almost welcome our intervention and visits. Charlotte had been observing all the activity with great interest, and as she obviously needed to be near Victoria we divided the stable into two, and there she sat watching Victoria for the next four days. On checking once again one evening we found Charlotte surrounded by seven lovely brown piglets. It was all most satisfactory and we had the greatest fun watching the little piglets run about, growing bigger and stronger every day. They were so curious and inquisitive, and we took some photographs of them at that time, making friends with dogs and donkeys.

Since 1985 Charlotte and Victoria have ruled the roost in the woods. The pigs are completely free; we feed them every morning, and apart from that they spend their time happily rooting round and living an entirely natural life. We allowed them to have a further four litters each and have usually kept one pig back from each litter. So now there is a little herd of wiggies in the woods, but we have to be far more careful now when going down to feed them. Recently we climbed into the woods with a bucket of apples and were immediately surrounded by fifteen half-grown and fully-grown pigs, and as soon as we started throwing the apples out we were almost submerged under a squealing, grunting mass, demonstrating that they preferred apples to anything else. We had to beat a hasty retreat to the fence which we vaulted over with an agility which totally belied our ages! It was rather difficult to try and look dignified as we walked up the field towards a group of donkey supporters who had viewed the proceedings with some amusement from the safety of the Sanctuary walk!

Apart from the pigs, I also purchased five Jacobs sheep from Mrs Judith Forbes when she ran Farway Countryside Park. Sheep and donkeys can live very well together. In fact from a health point of view sheep are essential in the management of fields where donkeys are to graze. The parasites affecting donkeys do not affect sheep and so when donkeys have been moved from a specific field the sheep are allowed in to graze off the grass and, of course, this destroys the parasite eggs laid in the grass from the donkeys' droppings. The little group of Jacobs that I purchased, which included one ram, wasted no time in starting to produce a family, and, as seems to be the case with everything I look after, things developed very fast. The sheep have adequate grazing and of course extra feed when needed, and the conditions provided seem to suit them down to the ground. The flock has now grown to approximately 160 and the wool produced provides an extra source of income for the Donkey Sanctuary, as in exchange for their keep

DERVOCK DONKEY MET NEXT OF KIN

Farmer, author, poet, wag, humorist and raconteur James G. Kenny of Ballygarvey, which is up there in the wilds beyond Ballymena, has been inveigled out of the shadows of an unusually long silence to recount a tale of the late Rev R. J. McIlmoyle of the Reformed Presbyterian Church who was known far and wide as a story-teller *par excellence*.

Before repeating that story, the Kenny boy, who is not short of more than a titter of wit either, says it was a real tragedy that the clergyman's repertoire was never recorded. James recalls: The best one ever to come from Mr McIlmoyle was about an old donkey which had wandered around Dervock for a day or two, probably abandoned by gypsies who realised its travelling days were done.

Finally, in the manse grounds, it croaked.

R. J. called at the police barracks in the vain hope that he could pass the buck but the sergeant, not void of a degree of sarcasm, said: 'I thought it was a minister's business to bury the dead.'

'I know,' came the swift reply, 'but I felt it was my duty to inform the next of kin.'

From *Belfast Newsletter*, December 2nd, 1989

Have you heard the one about the donkey stallion who brought a BBC film crew to its knees? Mistook the soundman's Afghan coat for a lady donkey and tried to mount a TV spectacular: – *Betty Svendsen, Devonshire's doyen of the donkey quoted by Susan Thomas, the* Guardian.

From *Sporting Life*, March 9th, 1984

One of the staff was in severe muscular pain all day. Thinking he had pulled a muscle in his shoulder, he decided when he got home to have a hot bath – only to find on removing his clothes that when dressing that morning he had put his arm through the neck of his vest!

the sheep pay their way with their wool. Many of them have grown very affectionate over the years and it's surprising how long they can live (twelve to fourteen years) when they're allowed to grow old instead of being produced for meat and sent off to market in their prime.

Also on the Sanctuary we have many goats who have been sent in as companions to donkeys, and these goats seem to settle happily even in large groups of donkeys. It can be quite distracting to walk into a barn with 200 donkeys standing happily taking hay from the feeders, and to find two or three goats totally unconcerned walking along inside the feeders, hopping from feeder to feeder and up on the straw bales which are sometimes stored at the sides of the barn.

An Apple a Day

An apple a day keeps the vet away
At least that's what I've heard,
But I only get an apple a week
Which to me is quite absurd.

In winter I've oats and hay every day
And a warm and cosy stall.
In summer I graze with the sheep, over there,
But they don't like apples at all.

I really don't mind, I'll eat any kind
Of apple that's offered to me,
It's the one thing I crave, so, if I behave
Can I try one a day? Please agree.

Margaret Riley

Other rescued friends include battery hens; I'm appalled by the way hens are kept in battery cages, and the comments of the owners that they must be happy because of all the 'clucking' noises they make during the day leaves me absolutely unconvinced. Occasionally when batteries are being cleared out and the birds sent for slaughter we are able to buy the contents of two or three cages. This usually means 15 hens. We are told that the inclination to scratch has been bred out of the hens and they have been perfectly happy to sit on metal bars for the whole of their lives to date.

When we get them back to the Sanctuary we have a special hen box to put them in, consisting of quite a large floor area with perches at low levels. Plenty of straw is spread on the ground and this is essential, as at this stage the hens' claws are perhaps 2½ to 3 inches long, completely soft, and white in colour. These need to start wearing down by walking, and this cannot be done overnight. On arrival, when we lift the poor hens out of the transporter box, they are totally unable to walk and just tend to flop down, sometimes on top of each other, and sit miserably looking around. After two or three days they begin to move a little on their own and within two or three weeks they are able to walk round on a hard surface pecking at food and beginning to enjoy their freedom.

At the end of the first month they are allowed to start wandering freely round the Sanctuary premises, and to see them actually scratching in the grass and digging up worms and beginning to live the normal life of poultry is most rewarding. During the night for at least the first three or four months we have to shut the hens in at night for their own safety against local foxes. However, they very soon regain their natural instincts and during the evenings fly up into the rafters for safety, generally using a donkey's back as a halfway jumping point! Once they are completely acclimatized these hens have the freedom of the whole Sanctuary and give a lot of pleasure and entertainment to our many visitors. They lay eggs all over the place, and most of them hatch. For the first time in their lives they are able to find real joy in living and to regain all the natural bird instincts that have been so cruelly denied them.

Beside my house I now have a large aviary; I hate to see birds in cages. I have an arrangement with the authorities at Heathrow through the Veterinary Department. Birds that have been imported illegally into the country and are caught by customs and impounded are then placed in quarantine by Government officials. Of these I am able to take the very small finches and other species that cannot be sold, and give them a home for the rest of their lives. I get the most enormous pleasure from rescuing these tiny terrified birds. I have also become known locally as occasionally I have to purchase a bird to pair up a single which is pining, and on my tours through the pet shops in the area I have been presented with many unsaleable birds, including one small group of five strawberry finches described as 'oven ready' by the dealer! They didn't have a feather between them, having been pecked almost to death in transit. It's been the most marvellous experience to see these tiny little birds gradually restored to full health and beautiful plumage and able to fly freely and safely in the big aviary. Many of the birds that I get are totally unable to fly for many days, having been cramped in tiny boxes, cages or suitcases for so long. My intensive care aviaries, all of which have thermostatically controlled heaters and dimmer switch lighting, are specially fitted so that there are tree branches from six inches up from the floor, and trees placed all around the aviary so that, as the birds can gradually fly a little bit more each day, they always have a perch on

DELILAH SCALES MORE HEIGHTS

Donkey Delilah is on top of the world, having conquered the highest peaks in England and Scotland to raise funds for the Ashbourne area youth clubs.

Accompanied by youth workers Hazel Wallis and Alan Fitchett, Delilah climbed Scafell Pike in the Lake District and Ben Nevis, having already scaled Snowdon on an earlier trip.

This second trip was not without incident. Conditions on Scafell Pike were so bad that Hazel had to scout ahead at times to make sure that it was safe to continue. Alan recalled that it was blowing a gale on the top and raining horizontally with very poor visibility which accounted for the amazement on the face of one elderly walker they encountered on the top looming out of the murk.

Completing the journey in seven hours included squeezing Delilah through a kissing gate.

The next day they travelled up to Scotland and after a mix-up over accommodation the local police helped them find a comfortable barn to camp in. They planned to have a day off the next day but the weather was fine and they pressed on to the summit, enjoying a fine view from the top before return-ing footsore but triumphant within the space of eight hours.

Hazel reported: 'When we got to Scotland Delilah was obviously pleased at the prospect of another walk, but we had to stop so many times to explain what we were doing that it took us longer than expected. She seemed to enjoy the trip very much.'

This is their last long distance outing of the season and Hazel hopes to have raised about £200 for local youth clubs.

From *Ashbourne News Telegraph*, October 1st, 1987

which to land. The pleasure of eventually seeing them make the topmost branches, knowing that they are going to be able to be released into the first small flying area of the aviary, is incredible. Once they have ventured into the small controlled area outside what has been their haven for the last few weeks, I am then able to open the door into the main large aviary, and see them free at last, able to fly at full pelt and make their own choice of perching and roosting — this is indeed a great pleasure.

Don't Tell Me What I Can Do

Recently Brian Bagwell, my Deputy, who'd had an extremely trying day and was feeling very uptight, was accosted just outside the office by an equally agitated John Rabjohns, the farm manager.

'Quick, Mr Bagwell,' he said, 'there's been an accident up on the corner and the trailer is stuck alongside a big posh car.'

Brian raced out with him and within a few minutes was at the scene. Three or four of our staff were desperately trying to rock the car in order to lever it away from the side of the trailer which was completely jammed against a smart, sleek, shining Alfa Romeo. As Deputy Administrator, Brian immediately took

19

command of the situation.

'Stop rocking that vehicle,' he said, after weighing everything up. 'What we are going to do', he continued, as the men gathered round, 'is to cut away that part of the trailer, as the metal ring is jammed right inside the door handle recess of the car.'

John Rabjohns immediately stepped forward, saying, 'You can't do that, Mr Bagwell.'

But before he had time to continue, Brian said, 'Don't tell me what I can do and what I can't do. That is what we are going to do and I'm going to get someone to saw this part of the trailer away.'

Without further ado Brian stormed off to find one of the carpenters working at the Sanctuary and returned a short while later.

It took about ten minutes to saw away part of the trailer and to Brian's great relief his plan worked and the Alfa Romeo was free.

'There,' said Brian, looking triumphantly at John, 'don't tell me we can't do that. There's your answer.'

'Mr Bagwell,' said John quietly, 'I didn't mean you couldn't do that, but it isn't our trailer, I've just borrowed it from our neighbour. You've just sawn up our neighbour's trailer.' As you can imagine our staff enjoyed this joke for some time, but I'm not so sure about the neighbour!

MULES AND HINNIES

Recently I found myself in conversation with a very elderly gentleman who knew a lot about mules, animals with which I have had little or no personal experience, and whose habits I only know through hearsay such as their reputation for obstinacy.

This dear old boy, however, had had a wealth of experience with mules, mainly during the First World War when he had come to hold them in high regard. In fact, he assured me that a lot of the men in France preferred them to horses because, in a curious way, they helped to boost morale. A mule, it seems, would remain quite unperturbed when a shell burst nearby whereas a horse would shy with fright.

I asked about the animal's traditional obstinacy and he agreed that this was not entirely without foundation although it was more a kind of built-in appreciation of its own limitations.

When a mule is required to pull a load it will put itself to the test by taking the strain to see how heavy it is. If it considers· the weight is too much, nothing on earth will induce it to move. In all normal circumstances, however, a mule will behave quite reasonably.

I was interested to hear that in one respect a mule resembles an elephant in that 'it never forgets'. I gather there have been a number of occasions when a mule that has been badly treated has got its own back on the individual concerned by lashing out with its hind legs, even though this may be some weeks later when the two happen to meet up again.

A mule is the result of a male donkey mating with a mare. If the mating takes place the other way round, in other words a stallion is the father and a female donkey the mother, the result is a hinny.

This is a much rarer occurrence and the end-product is far less satisfactory as a hinny is too small and weak to serve the interests of man.

What can never happen, I am assured, is for a mule and a hinny to produce offspring of their own.

Eric Roberts
From *Exeter Express and Echo,*
January 25th, 1990

Putting My Foot in it!

Losing one's partner is always a traumatic time and shortly after my marriage ended I booked a holiday to St Lucia in the West Indies to try and get away from everything and take a much needed break. June Evers went with me, and we really had a very enjoyable time. However, being full of energy, I soon found lying on a beach wasn't really enough for me and I was drawn to a yacht-hire company, where I tried to make arrangements to rent a yacht. The plan was to sail over to Martinique, an island lying close to St Lucia. I managed to get this all agreed with the yacht charterers, and I turned round to see a vaguely familiar figure standing behind me.

He immediately accosted me saying, 'You're not going to take a boat on your own across to Martinique, just you two ladies, are you?'

I said, 'Yes, most certainly I am. Why do you ask?'

'Well,' he said, 'it isn't easy taking a yacht and you need somebody with experience.'

By the time I had explained the years of yachting I'd done with my husband and my ability to cope, he had become much more affable and in fact suddenly surprised me by saying, 'Don't I know you? I'm sure I've met you before,' and within a very short time I realized that I was talking to Ted Bull who had been my son's commanding officer in the RAF and who, in fact, had sailed with my son in 'Black Arrow' in some of the competitions we had all taken part in. Meeting Ted was enormously helpful for me; he was great fun and the rest of the holiday passed very rapidly.

Ted had told me he was due to come over to England about three months later and so I agreed to meet him at the Southampton Boat Show and arranged that he would visit my house and the Donkey Sanctuary on his way down to his sister in Cornwall. All should have gone well, were it not for the fact that going out to the donkeys one afternoon I stumbled over a stone and unfortunately broke my ankle. I was actually sitting on the ground wondering how I was going to manage to get up and get back to the office, when two visitors just going round the Sanctuary approached me and held quite a long conversation with me about the Donkey Sanctuary before wandering off again to look around, never asking why I was sitting on the ground and why I didn't attempt to get up! By the time they had gone, I was in considerable pain and was extremely pleased when John Rabjohns, our farm manager, walked along and immediately realized I wasn't sitting there just to chat to the visitors. I was whisked off to hospital where I was put in plaster.

Being plastered was no joke – even being off my feet was no joke, with the work that had to be done both indoors and out at the Sanctuary, so I asked if they would put a rocker at the bottom of the plaster which would enable me to walk on the plaster rather than having to use crutches, and this they obligingly did. The rocker caused me immense problems. I suppose I walked on it (a) too soon and (b) too much, because twice I had to go back to have it strengthened, but by the time the Southampton Boat Show arrived I was feeling much more agile and able to cope. As agreed, I met Ted in Southampton, Brian Bagwell, my Deputy, having driven me there as driving was out of the question. Ted Bull was going to bring me home.

We had a super time at the show until we decided to go down onto the pontoons where you could board the boats and look at the various classes. To my horror the rocker just managed to fit into the slats of the pontoon and my very first step onto the walkway ended in near disaster. The rocker wedged firmly between the planks and I was completely stuck and unable to move. I must say I found the situation rather embarrassing after a while; they had to close the pontoon bridge to stop more people coming down, as I had caused a complete jam and nobody was able to get around me or lever me out of my problem. After a great deal of effort, pushing and pulling, and with the aid of three chisels they eventually prised the planks open wide enough for me to get my foot out, and a by then rather red-faced Ted Bull suggested that we make our way back to the car and drive back to Devon.

Donkeys have such expressive faces.

The rocker on my foot was by this time completely loose and of no value to me whatsoever. Ted, however, is a very practical man and we stopped at the first big garage we saw and he reappeared from the garage shop clutching a tin called 'bodyfiller'. As soon as we got back home he got to work mixing up this bodyfiller which after a few seconds was guaranteed to set hard. The bodyfiller was coloured a bright red and with great care Ted mixed it all up, and with me lying on the end of the settee with my foot stuck over the edge and newspapers liberally spread underneath, he refitted my rocker by slapping the bodyfiller generously over the plaster cast. This really was a success; from the time it set, which took about five minutes, I had no more problems.

At least, not until the day I went back to Wonford Hospital, Exeter. Whilst waiting in the queue of patients to have the cast removed, two men sitting near me were discussing their 'rockers', both of which were loose; one was saying it was his third visit back. I proudly showed them my bodyfiller cast and they were greatly impressed and in fact both left before going in to have their plasters reset, bound for the nearest garage to get some bodyfiller. When my turn came to have my plaster taken off I found a rather irritated elderly gentleman assigned to my cast. He took one horrified look at it and said, 'What on earth have you done to your cast?' I explained that the rocker kept coming off and that my friend had done it with bodyfiller. He snorted at me, 'In that case your friend had better come and take it off, because none of the equipment I've got here will do that.' With that he marched out of the cubicle. I waited rather pensively for about another twenty minutes and nobody came near, so I attracted the attention of a passing nurse and asked her what was happening.

She said, 'You've really caused a stir. I don't think we've anything here that will get through bodyfiller,' and off she went.

An hour later I was still sitting there. Fortunately June Evers, my friend, was Superintendent of Radiography at Exeter Hospital and I asked one of the nurses if she would phone through to X-ray and ask June if she could spare some time to come down. I had never been so pleased to see June as when she walked into my cubicle. Apart from the fact that she was half convulsed with laughter at the furore I was causing in the department, she explained they were trying to get some special equipment down from theatre which was being used to cut through steel and that they would be down shortly to try and do something for me. For the next two hours June stayed whilst they tried circular saws and various other equipment, finally having to go down to the local garage to obtain some special cutting equipment which removed the offending plaster. I felt extremely guilty as I left the hospital and very grateful that it was all over.

But as fate would have it, within two weeks I was pushed rather hard by an over-friendly donkey and in saving my right ankle, which was still very weak, I put all my weight on the left ankle and fell over, to my horror breaking my left ankle! I was rather quiet as I was taken into the hospital, wondering who was going to be on duty and how they would react to my visit so soon after the previous disaster. I can't say I was encouraged when I sat waiting to be treated and found the two gentlemen who had been with me two weeks before, sitting proudly with their casts covered in red bodyfiller! This time I didn't even wait to go in, but sent a desperate call through to June who came down to help me once again, and made quite sure I got different staff to attend to me this time, keeping me well clear of the repeat performance of trying to remove plaster casts strongly bonded by the automobile trade!

From Gardener to Area Welfare Officer

It was a beautiful Sunday morning in July and we were gathered on the small back lawn of our house. I was looking at the fish in the pond when Mrs S (or 'Mother' as she is known, not only to the staff, but also to many Sanctuary visitors) arrived. After a while Mrs S asked if I might like to write a chapter for a new book; nothing extraordinary about that, you may think, but for me it was a huge lift from the depression I was in.

Just seven days earlier, on Monday, July 9th, 1990, I had been told that I had cancer and could expect to live for only 6-12 months. Needless to say I felt utter and total despair; the whole world seemed to crash around me. My wife had been waiting outside the oncologist's room, and I told her the bad news, trying very hard not to cry. Back at home later that day we were both visited by Mary, the Macmillan nurse. This meeting had been arranged by Brian Bagwell who had driven Judy and I to the hospital and back again. We decided that together we could fight it; we would prove the doctors wrong. Cancer can be beaten and I was going to do just that.

As the next few days went by I found out how supportive family, friends and work colleagues could be, yet even with this support I soon realized that it was not going to be easy to keep my spirits up all of the time. I kept going into black pits of depression, as I was on that Sunday morning when Mrs S arrived.

I don't know if it was intentional or not, but her usual magic worked when she made her request for me to produce this chapter. She had given me the incentive I needed, a target, something to reach for. I know we were only talking about a single chapter in one book, but to me at that moment it was as important as *Great Expectations* must have been to Charles Dickens or *Gone with the Wind* to Margaret Mitchell.

I became a member of the Sanctuary staff during October 1984. I knew absolutely nothing about donkeys and was not even expected to. My employment was as the Sanctuary gardener. In a short while, and I like to think it wasn't obvious, I started to find many gardening jobs that just happened to be next door to a stable or run-out yard containing donkeys. Learning the names and the histories of the donkeys became much more fun than cutting grass or pulling weeds. If a visitor should ask me a question about the Sanctuary or a particular donkey, I had the answers right at once, and I was very proud of this. I still thought that no one was noticing

Neil Harvey hugging a donkey.

how little garden work was being accomplished! I was wrong. It was noticed, and on more than one occasion I stood before Mother and the farm manager making excuses about what had not been done or what should have been done, and had to explain that I was not trying to do the 'show-round' staff out of their rightful employment! Of course this couldn't last, and it didn't.

A vacancy came up for the position of second lorry driver; I asked for the job and got it. At last I no longer had to pretend that I was doing something else whilst all the time wanting to be with the donkeys. Now my job meant I had to be with them. The second lorry driver's job was basically to move donkeys between farms as and when necessary, and carry out any emergency work that the main lorry was unable to cope with. Between driving, I helped out with general farm work as directed by the managers. Those were the times when I felt I got to know donkeys; by this I don't mean by name, such as 'this is Eeyore, that one is Pedro', but I seemed to gain an understanding of the way they thought, what they needed or how they would react to any given situation. Yes, both donkeys and I decided we really did like each other and we were going to get along just fine.

I was soon to learn that not everything was to have a happy ending. 'Stepping Out' and 'Dinky' were foals born during Donkey Week in 1985, and with 300 donkey lovers at the Sanctuary the

25

numbers of 'oohs' and 'aahs' were countless. Dinky had been fine and had shown no cause for any concern, but as I passed the stable where he and his mother were, I looked over the door at him, and stopped. Dinky was then three days old; he was resting on a straw bed, but I felt that something wasn't right; nothing obvious, but there was something. I called the vet and went about my own business. Mrs S spoke to me just as we were all finishing the day's work. She told me that Dinky was really ill and she wanted someone to sit with him in the hospital while the vet and nurses treated him. This I did, but despite everything being done for him Dinky died at 9 p.m. At that moment only Dinky and I were in the hospital box, and he went quietly in his sleep. I learnt two things that night; this job did have its sad moments, and grown men do cry.

During November I went on my first 'emergency' donkey collection. One of our supporters living in Northampton had discovered 9 miniature donkeys living in grounds belonging to an old lady. They were not cruelty cases, but were simply neglected. In fact the owner thought she had only 7 donkeys; 2 foals had been born which she wasn't aware of! I arrived at the premises at 4.30 p.m. and parked the lorry in the stable yard of the lovely old house. Whilst waiting for the lady who had reported the donkeys I looked around, and found a miniature stallion who was shut in one of the stables, with two mares and foals in another. Apparently our supporter, Mrs Clarke, and her husband had spent some time catching and stabling them ready for collection, but somewhere were another 4 donkeys. Mr and Mrs Clarke arrived and explained how difficult it had been to catch the donkeys as they were living in a semi-wild state. By now it was pitch dark and bitterly cold as the three of us made our way out of the yard and into the field. The field must have been at least twenty acres in size, not ideal for catching wild donkeys. Within an hour we had caught 3 and had stabled them back in the yard, but we had not even caught sight of the fourth one. The three captured donkeys had only one thing on their minds – eating – they couldn't believe their luck as we spread hay out in the feeders, and didn't stop eating all night. Mr and Mrs Clarke went home at 8.30 p.m. and agreed to return at first light the next morning.

I could find only crisps to eat in the village inn but by 10 p.m. I was back in the field, full of crisps, and by now it was bitterly cold with a heavy frost and freezing fog. I walked up and down that field for hours, realizing that, as the hedges were not in good condition, an animal could simply walk through into the surrounding fields. At 2 a.m. I still hadn't found the donkey and, feeling rather dejected, went back to the lorry to sleep. It was far too cold, and at 5 a.m. I was back in the field, and surrounded by the thick fog I almost

walked into the donkey. Absolutely delighted with myself, I slipped a head collar on her and walked back to the yard to stable her. No longer feeling the need to sleep I started to load the donkeys; Charlie the stallion first, followed by the mares and foals. The rest of the donkeys took a dislike to the lorry so I decided it would be best to delay loading them until the Clarkes arrived. When they arrived at 7.30 a.m., I pointed out rather pompously that all nine donkeys were in captivity.

From a Rescued Donkey

You came, you saw, you rescued me
And led me through the door.
To love, care and tenderness
I had never known before.

My coat is brushed, my feet are trimmed,
My eyes are bright and clear.
I really cannot quite believe
I need have no more fear.

I have seen some bad days,
The good ones stretch ahead.
I have the fields to graze in
And straw down for my bed.

I am one of many donkeys,
Whose plight changed overnight.
So here's my thanks to all of you
Who never give up the fight.

It took a while to give my trust
But you waited patiently.
Now all is well, I'll spend my life
Here, in this Sanctuary.

Peggy Judge

'No,' said Mrs Clarke, pointing at my last captive, 'that one isn't ours,' and pointing towards the field said, 'Ours is still out there somewhere.'

After drinking a welcome flask full of hot tea brought by the Clarkes, we trooped off again. At last I had my first sight of Harriet, who ran to the far end of the field as we approached. Whenever we got within 100 yards of her she ran off again and I'm quite sure that we must all have run three or four miles in an hour. Eventually Harriet made the mistake of going through a broken fence into an overgrown garden, where we cornered her and, having put a head collar on, we all went back to the lorry. I began the return journey to the Sanctuary at 9.30 a.m. It had taken a total of seventeen hours to catch and load the nine donkeys, which has to be the most difficult and longest donkey-loading job I have ever undertaken. If you are ever at the Sanctuary ask about the 'Manor' donkeys; you will not believe that such small donkeys could cause so much of a problem.

Sometime later I was asked to Mother's office, and when she offered me the job of looking after the isolation donkeys I accepted at once. Isolation is perhaps the most critical time for any donkey coming into the Sanctuary, and extra special care and individual attention must be given to each donkey to help settle into Sanctuary life. It is always easier for the neglected donkey to settle with us, as suddenly he finds that food is plentiful, kind voices and cuddles are limitless, he has a warm bed and a dry stable, and because this is so new and wonderful it doesn't matter that the vet occasionally sticks a needle in somewhere! The donkey that has come from a caring home, however, sometimes finds that Sanctuary life can be a little stressful at the beginning. You can imagine what it's like; he has had a kind owner and friend for twenty years or more, and then for one reason or another he finds himself in the back of a lorry and transported away from everything he has ever known, from safety, kindness and the place and person he has loved. It's not possible to explain to him that he is going to a place where people are just as kind and he will be just as secure and loved every bit as much as he has been used to. What we can do is demonstrate our care and love to him, but unfortunately some donkeys take longer to realize this than others, and these have to be watched very carefully, given lashings of tender loving care and reassurance. A knowledge of how the donkey thinks is essential at these times, otherwise hyperlipaemia may set in. Hyperlipaemia is a condition whereby fat reserves in the body liquefy and enter the bloodstream, and this means that clots or globules of fat can form, with possibly fatal results.

As time went on my occupation within the Sanctuary regularly changed. Promotion of course is always welcome and promotion within the Sanctuary is like the icing on the cake, because one already has the best job in the world. I became Senior Lorry Driver, Deputy Farm Manager and then Area Welfare Officer for the South of England and Wales. The following stories in this chapter are taken from all aspects of my Sanctuary career, and, short though they may be, I hope they give a little flavour of Sanctuary life.

One incident concerns two donkeys named Spot and Miss White. Spot had been sent into the Sanctuary as a single donkey, and, as is normal, two or three days after arrival she had a

complete medical from the vets and was passed fully fit. But was she? As the days went on it became obvious that something was drastically wrong. Physically she was fine, but she was very unhappy and it came to the stage where Mother was extremely concerned for her. The Sanctuary's Welfare Department had been

Once a Sad Donkey

My hooves were long and curly, my coat was harsh and dry,
My sores were very many and I wished that I might die;
My master was a bully who beat me every day;
He told me I was lazy and he would make me pay.

How I longed to have some respite, a few kindly words to hear,
Some pats and some encouragement to give my days some cheer,
I couldn't ever please him, for however much I tried
He made me work the harder whatever did betide.

If only he had liked me, just a little, so to speak,
I could have moved the world for him and still been quiet and meek.
The man was never satisfied and never did he say –
'Well done, my little donkey, you have worked well today.'

I struggled on and did my best until one sorry day
I fell and could not rise again to work nor yet to play.
It really seemed my end had come, I felt so very ill;
But help came in the nick of time whilst life was in me still.

A loving lady came to me and took me clear away;
Soft kind voices spoke to me and misery gave way,
Hope dawned in sleepy cadences as wearily I lay
And slowly, very slowly, care drove all hurt away.

See now, I'm really happy and just love living here,
My coat is soft and shining and my eyes are bright and clear.
My hooves are trimmed and neat again, that took some doing, aye,
It was a long long time before I could leap towards the sky.

And now each day I wake to find companions dear to me.
We play and graze and stand about most contentedly.
They call this place a sanctuary and I don't know what that means
But to me it's a donkey's heaven and it fulfils all my dreams.

Felicia M. Carran

put to work by this time and by tracing Spot's history they found the answer. She hadn't been a single donkey at all but had been separated from a donkey called Miss White. We managed to trace her to a home in Kent and the new owners agreed for her to come to Devon to comfort Spot. We made immediate plans for the journey. Restrictions on driving hours as well as the need to bring Miss White back to the Sanctuary as quickly as possible meant that both John Rabjohns and I set off in the lorry at 5 a.m. We collected Miss White and John and I arrived back at the Sanctuary at 4.30 p.m. It may seem unbelievable but Spot must have smelled or sensed that Miss White was on the lorry, because before we had undone the ramp she was going frantic at the fence of the isolation yard. When John led her off the lorry and they caught sight of each other, neither of us had heard anything like it before! The other donkeys looked on in amazement as Spot and Miss White raced round and round hee-hawing as loud as they could. Neither donkey nor human was allowed anywhere near Miss White, as Spot's hoofs ensured that no one was going to take her away again. Happily both donkeys thrived as time went on and both are now living on one of our Sanctuary farms. One thing is guaranteed; no one will ever try to split those two donkeys again!

On another occasion we had two drivers on one lorry in order to bring donkeys into the Sanctuary as quickly as possible. Mother called me to her office at 4 p.m., and explained the situation. An equine charity in Sussex had run into problems. There were 11 donkeys and a number of horses and ponies that had to be brought out by midnight, otherwise the bailiffs would be taking the animals, which implied that they would be slaughtered. By 4.30 p.m., Ray Mutter, the Slade Centre (the centre for handicapped children at the Sanctuary) Ambulance driver, and I were on our way to Sussex. We arrived at the troubled sanctuary at 9.30 p.m. A number of lorries were blocking the drive, so we parked and walked to the stables.

What a sight met us; the place was a complete shambles. The muck inside the stables was higher than the tops of our Wellington boots. The sooner the animals at this place were removed the better. The lorries blocking the drive belonged to various horse charities, and we assisted in loading up the horses and ponies, and waved them on their way. At least none of the animals was going for slaughter; there were over a hundred of them, and they were all going to new homes. By 10 p.m. we were able to load the 11 donkeys. It was hard to believe they had been living in a sanctuary; they were starving and didn't stop eating from the moment they entered the lorry. We arrived back in Devon at 4.30 a.m., and the donkeys walked into their isolation stables and carried on eating. Ray and myself, well pleased with the night's work, went looking for our beds. All the donkeys thrived with our care, and all are well and happy on one of our farms.

No doubt you all remember the great hurricane of October 1987 which hit the south-east of England. I certainly do as, when it hit, I was in the Brighton/Worthing area and had parked the lorry, with one donkey on board. It was the longest, most frightening night of my life. The dilemma was deciding where to park; out in the open and risk being blown over, or under a tree and perhaps have the tree on top of us! The situation resolved itself as another lorry pulled up alongside and in the layby there was a large container on a trailer. We parked broadside to this trailer so that we were three abreast. This action didn't prevent us from rocking around like ships at sea, but at least we would not get blown right over onto our sides. Frequent visits to the back of the lorry to check on the

---

Inspired by the work undertaken at the
Slade Farm Donkey Sanctuary
at Sidmouth in Devon

Sanctuary

What are you thinking behind those grey eyes?
What makes you sad and why those great sighs?
Are they thoughts of green pastures and life on a farm
Where you'll be protected and come to no harm?

The beach is deserted. They day's at an end.
Her back is near breaking, and who now will tend
the raw open sores on her feet and her sides
through twelve hours of working the tenpenny rides?

Yet this is the summer when times are not hard.
The torment is winter at work in the yard
on a broken-down car dump where jagged sharp steel
cuts into the flesh, with no time to heal.

We can hardly repay this unkindness of Man
with the gift of a carrot or handful of bran
but it's some consolation that there are just a few
who will offer their life and devotion to you.

Geoffrey Ford

---

donkey proved to be unnecessary, as she had only one thing in mind, which was to demolish the contents of her hay net. She may not have been concerned with the constant buffeting and crashing of trees and buildings, but I certainly was. When daylight came and the wind dropped it was an enormous relief. I looked around and the sight was unbelievable. How we survived without damage was a miracle. I had one more donkey to collect on the way home, so off we went, and my light-hearted report on the collection of this donkey appeared in our Spring 1988 Newsletter, as follows:

'Creeping past fallen trees had become boring. The interesting bits were getting around chimneys – still attached to their roofs – piles of bricks, garden sheds, lamp posts, a 25 foot cabin cruiser and electricity lines throwing blue sparks across the road. There must have been a lot of boundary disputes going on, because many people appeared to have erected their garden walls and fences down the middle of the road! At Arundel, complete blockage – time to make coffee. This was a foolish move in an area without electricity. Twenty minutes and 15 or 16 cups later, I ran out of milk and was only able to supply black tea and coffee. I don't know what onlookers must have thought when they saw my lorry in the middle of a roundabout dispensing hot tea or coffee to all and sundry – just like a mobile cafe!

'An hour later we were all directed on to the scenic route via Bognor Regis. It seemed the local council had a policy of placing their road signs face downwards in the mud, but by adopting a policy of 'people pay good money for mystery tours', one kept going along any road that was open. I knew I had arrived at Portsmouth, because the owner of 24 Shoreham Road said he was going to write to Portsmouth council for diverting the A27 across his front garden without first seeking permission! On arrival at West Meon, being told by the locals that I would never get to Whitelands because of fallen trees, my new-found sense of adventure took over. After a quick consultation of the map, I decided that if Mrs Smith moved her dustbin from her drive and Mrs Brown took down her washing line, there was bound to be enough unblocked back gardens, farm yards and patios to provide access to Whitelands. This proved to be correct, and only a fallen holly tree prevented me from getting any closer than 100 yards from the house, so it was a very surprised Mrs White who took me to the donkeys!'

An amusing little incident cannot go without mention. You have all seen those roadside caravans selling snacks and teas. One day whilst in the Midlands I decided to stop for a cup of tea at one of these snack bars and, walking over to the van, I could see two faces staring open-mouthed at the lorry from the serving hatch. Before I could open my mouth, one lady said, 'The Donkey Sanctuary – that's been on the telly, hasn't it?' 'Yes, several times,' I answered. I was presented with a cup of tea, a bacon sandwich and a £2 donation, with the words 'Cor, we've never had anybody famous stop here before!' Perks indeed!

One of the saddest yet happiest tales I can think of concerns Jack Wormleighton and his donkey, Butch. Jack was nearly 80 years old and kept Butch in his large back garden on the outskirts of Leicester. Jack had owned Butch from a six-month-old foal, for 25 years. Never had I seen such a relationship between man and animal; they absolutely adored each other. Such was Jack's concern for Butch that, if it snowed, Jack would put four socks on Butch's feet. Jack realized that age was against him in so far as he could not care for Butch in the same manner as he had in the past,

Jack and Butch enjoying the sunshine together.

so he asked us to take Butch in.

I arrived at Jack's home in the afternoon, and I knew this wasn't going to be a normal collection when Jack gave me a suitcase and told me it contained Butch's belongings. He had tears in his eyes, for which he apologized, saying that he was losing his mate. I opened the back of the lorry and I think for the only time I let the owner load his own donkey. Jack did not want to get out of the lorry, so I left them together for about half an hour. I will always be convinced that, when I returned, not only Jack had tears in his eyes but Butch did too. It took me a long time to convince Jack that it wasn't necessary for him to ride to the Sanctuary in the back of the lorry. Even I needed a handkerchief as I drove away, and you may wonder how this turned out to be a happy tale. Well, Jack comes down to the Sanctuary three or four times a year to visit Butch and all the other donkeys. Butch has happily settled into Sanctuary life and Jack has made many new friends.

I do hope these little stories will give you a taste of what sanctuary life can bring to a member of staff. I hesitate to refer to the Sanctuary as a place of work; it isn't work, it's a way of life 'down among the donkeys'.

Neil Harvey
He died on October 13th, 1990

And So Say All of Us

'My day starts at 7 a.m. and every morning as I enter the yards a loud chorus of 'hee-haws' rings out. The first job is to feed the donkeys with hay and straw and to make sure each barn has clean fresh bedding. The yards are scraped clean every day and the dung piled into a big pit. This work usually takes us most of the morning and for the rest of the day there is the field work to do, such as ditching, fencing, hedging, etc. On wet days we spend our time grooming the donkeys.'

John Axe, Farm Worker, Three Gates Farm

'As Chief Inspector for the Donkey Sanctuary, Ireland, I am responsible for the welfare of the abandoned and mistreated donkeys here. I work in close liaison with the Gardai as without their help it would be very difficult to do the job. I am also responsible for the five voluntary inspectors who are doing a great job assisting me in caring for the donkeys throughout the country.

'My job also involves farm management. I am assisted by Gerry, when he is not delivering and collecting donkeys. My wife, Eileen, daughters Helen and Debbie, also help out on the farm. There are always between 60 and 70 donkeys here. They are sorted out into different groups – isolation group, the young healthy active group, the older group which require extra care and attention and the rehabilitation group where the donkeys are groomed daily and handled, preparing them for new homes. I also make appointments for veterinary and farriery visits. My working day varies each week and I am always on call.

'When people visit the Sanctuary at weekends and late evenings, I take them around the farm to meet the donkeys. I like my job very much. It gives me great satisfaction to see the rescued donkeys that come here, some grossly emaciated, badly injured, and with very overgrown feet, brought back to good health.'

Paddy Barrett, Chief Welfare Officer, Ireland

'I work in one of the most exciting and dynamic parts of the Sanctuary – which is, of course, the Accounts Department! Words are barely adequate to describe the fascinating events that daily take place. On Monday morning my first stimulating task is doing the wages. The scope for enterprise and initiative here is remarkable, as I contemplate the computer screen knowing that the mere slip of a finger on the keyboard can mean the difference between poverty and a week of luxury for some (un)fortunate member of the staff. As I near the end of a morning of intense concentration, the adrenalin is really flowing and my pulse is racing as I try to ensure that Tom gets the right number of travelling days and Dick has his holiday pay.

'Of course once a month it is also salary time as well as wages and this means it all goes on for much longer and there's a lot more of it.'

Heather Brown, Accounts Department

An Intelligent Ass

There was an old donkey called Ned,
Who took to wearing glasses,
Often reading when in bed
A rarity in asses.

Ned relished tales about a horse,
Whose capers made him laugh.
His favourite papers were, of course,
The Times, *and* Telegraph.

Ned had a way with nursery rhymes,
His style was quite unique
He did the crossword in the Times,
Wrote comic-verse in Greek.

Yet Ned remained a modest beast
Even when renowned
Carrots were to him a feast
On caviar he frowned.

Ned lived to be a ripe old age
Wondrous wise and witty
Perusing books from page to page
Whiling time with ditty.

Unhappily one Hogmanay
Just after food and wine
Ned's lively spirit passed away
While singing Auld-Lang-Syne.

They buried him beneath the grass
These words above his head
'Here lies an intellectual ass
Who loved to read in bed.'

John Howard Bennett

'My job hasn't really changed since I joined Mrs Svendsen in October 1974 – I was interviewed whilst she fed and groomed two pathetic new arrivals – Hansel and Gretal.

'The Sanctuary has grown – Slade Centre, IDPT (International Donkey Protection Trust) and now EST (Elisabeth Svendsen

The Donkey Sanctuary

On the south coast of Devon
Where the hills run down to the sea,
And the grass is green on the gentle slopes,
Is the Donkey Sanctuary.

They are happy there in the pure fresh air,
For these are the lucky ones
Who have a kind and loving home
Safe from the knacker's guns.

These were 'despised and rejected of men'
And they carry the Cross on their backs.
And they know man's inhumanity and greed.
Yes; every Jenny and Tommy and Max
Has a story to tell of hurt and neglect,
Of cruelty and suffering and pain.
But now, here in Devon, here on this farm
They begin to be happy again.

The donkeys that I knew when I was a girl
Each carried a child on its back
Up and down on the sands. We knew all their names.
There was Snowie, and Darkie, and Jack.
They worked for their keep, and their keeper was kind,
They had shelter, and food in their sheds,
At the end of the day when their working was done
And we children were all in our beds.

But these had been starved, ill-treated and sad.
They were sick, and close to despair.
I wonder what joy they feel in their hearts
Now they're here, with the people who care?

For here at the farm they have all that they need.
There's a nursery, and hospital too.
And when they've been tended, and nursed back to health
There's something they're able to do
For the handicapped children, who come here to ride
Or go out in the trap, or just play.
They ride in procession, in triumph and joy;
As our Lord rode a donkey one day.

I went there and saw them, and walked round the farm.
And I watched the procession pass by;
With some children on donkeys and some in the trap;
When I was in Devon – in July.

Mrs Ellen M. Summers

Trust), a donkey hospital, ten farms, annual Donkey Weeks, festivals every two years and a large efficient Welfare Department which works throughout England, Scotland, Wales and Ireland.

'Now I am the Assistant Administrator and in 1974 I was a "do anything, catch that donkey" secretary but not much has changed apart from having been one of three staff then and now being one of 150. My job covers the smooth running of the office and the Information Centre. I have a great interest in the Welfare Department, visit our Lamu Sanctuary annually and help at the Slade Centre when needed. I know a little about everything – well, you would after 16 years if you loved your job. It is said "a little knowledge is a bad thing": oh dear, mine spans talks about our charities to WIs, etc., donkeys' names, history and owners (I don't know as many now, as we have over 4,500 donkeys), computers, tea machines, stationery, office machinery, uniforms, light bulbs, daily post, newsletters, whereabouts of donkeys, memory plaques, visitors (many of our regulars are now old friends) and whether the offices and loos are clean, just to name a few.'

Julie Policutt-Courtney, Assistant Administrator

'I love working out of doors, especially with the donkeys because I never realized how loving and wonderful donkeys really are! Compared with all the other sorts of animals I have worked with, donkeys need a lot more love and attention.'

Tony Downs, Brookfield Farm

'My duties are to visit, assist and supervise my Voluntary Welfare Officers. We carry out investigations into complaints of cruelty, carry out self-initiated investigations, attend horse sales and fairs, donkey derbys, give advice and guidance to donkey owners, liaise

NOW LISTEN EAR, MUM

Champers is only seven days old, and he is already bending mum's ears about how good life is at the donkey sanctuary at Salcombe Regis, near Sidmouth. His mum, Tina, is really proud of this little colt because he's the 4,000th resident of the sanctuary. Tina came to the sanctuary because her previous owner couldn't afford to keep her.
From *Pulman's Weekly News*, July 27th, 1989

closely with local authority officers, police, RSPCA, veterinary surgeons and other equine charities. Other duties involve visiting our rehab donkeys (rehomed donkeys) on regular visits.'

Bert Duncan, Chief Welfare Officer, Midlands Area

Poem to a Lady about to be Decorated

The tall, the small,
The fat, the thin.
Still the donkeys
Kept coming in.

More farms were bought
And workers taught.
Then of course,
The money was short.

'Help our donkeys'
Came the plea
In papers, letters
And on TV.

Soon old and young
And rich and poor
Sent pennies speeding
To the Sanctuary's door.

One day Maggie Thatcher heard,
And off to Buck House sent the word,
Betty Svendsen, MBE
We all send love – donkeys, staff and me.

Vanadia Sandon-Humphries

'Having worked for the Sanctuary for the past 16 years I have seen many changes, but the basic farming methods can never change, as all depends on "Mother Nature" and the weather. The donkeys are always brought into the yards and barns for the winter months and are allowed to roam around as one large group. Every month they are all weighed and any I am not happy with are put into a smaller group and given extra feed. In the spring the fields are rolled and chain harrowed to prepare for haymaking, which has to be made as good as possible, as this is the main source of feed throughout the winter. During the summer the donkeys are out in the fields, which means all fences have to be secure. The barns are then mucked out, steam cleaned and any repairs carried out. This is basically a 24-hour job – hard work, but the contentment of the donkeys makes it all worthwhile.'

John Fry, Farm Manager, Three Gates Farm

'The best part of the job is guiding parties of school children around the Sanctuary. They are happy and a little noisy on a day out and the donkeys love greeting them. It is especially satisfying to help to educate the coming generation to an understanding and love of animals and their needs. Most visitors are, or become, enthusiastic about the Sanctuary and it is a great pleasure to meet them. During the winter I am employed two or more days a week on what might seem mundane tasks but which, after a working lifetime in "the rat race", I enjoy: collating newsletters, counting and packing notelets and Christmas cards, stapling children's colouring books, helping with the despatch of mail and sometimes during school holidays back to my favourite employment in the Information Centre where I meet so many kind and interesting people.'

Sydney Judge, Office Clerk/Guide

'Correspondence takes part of my time and I answer general queries and acknowledge most of the fund-raising donations – the wide range of ways people do this for the donkeys is fascinating. Also I deal with "in memory" donations and arrange all the plaques on our Memory Wall and under trees, etc., throughout the Sanctuary. My other task is helping to organize Donkey Week and this extends over the whole year as far as I am concerned; starting in August when we talk to the hotels, getting details for printing in our Christmas newsletter. A lot of the festival correspondence falls

ROYAL PAT FOR BUFFALO

Buffalo, a retired Blackpool beach donkey, stole the heart of Princess Anne yesterday. The Princess, more usually associated with horses, made a beeline for Buffalo during a visit to the donkey sanctuary at Salcombe Regis, near Sidmouth.

Buffalo, at 39 one of the oldest and most popular animals at the sanctuary – thrust his head from his stall for a bit of Royal attention. He was not disappointed. The Princess smiled and patted him gently, to the delight of cameramen, while sanctuary founder Mrs Betty Svendsen told her the animal's history.

Buffalo spent most of his working life trudging up and down the sands of Blackpool before retiring to enjoy the good life at the sanctuary eight years ago.

Princess Anne, president of Riding for the Disabled, toured the sanctuary and the adjoining Slade Centre where disabled children are taught to ride.

Earlier, the Princess, recently made an honorary associate member of the Royal College of Veterinary Surgeons in recognition of her long-standing interest in veterinary matters, had made history when she opened the British Veterinary Association's annual congress at Exeter.

From *Western Morning News,* September 13th, 1985

FOUR-LEGGED STAR THAT LOVES PLAYING THE FOOL

Performers at the Port Talbot Passion Play, *Behold the Man*, are hoping one of its four-legged stars will keep tight lipped during its 12 night run at Margam Country Park.

Bandit is one of eight donkeys who reside at the park and he has appeared in Passion Plays for 10 years.

He has been known to bite a production assistant and has strayed into the audience with Jesus on his back.

'We are just hoping everything will be alright on the night,' said the secretary of the Port Talbot Passion Play Association, Mr Peter Davies.

Association chairman, Mr John Adams, who works at the park, said: 'Bandit has strayed away from his main role in the past, but we are hoping he will stick to the script this year or we will have to seriously consider getting a stand in.'

From *South Wales Evening Post*, May 1989

'Now this is your last chance to perform as an actor' – Bandit, the reluctant donkey, is given a face-to-face talk by Mr Rex Baddeley, Chief Ranger at Margam Park.

to me and, as I seem to attract jumble like a magnet, I end up helping on the jumble stall at the festival. I enjoy helping to show visitors round when necessary and meet lots of interesting people from all over the world. Many of our regular donors and visitors have become real friends, and this makes for tremendous job satisfaction.'

Diana Murray, Part-time Secretary

'Afternoon, my name be "Foreman" fer Brookfield Varm and I've toiled yer for nigh on 7½ yers under old Charley Courtney. Afore 'e got 'old of me, I was an 'erdsman, an so 'ave always been around animals and the like. 'Tis a perquliar life, 'aving spent manys a yer

43

looking at the backend of cows, to what I be doing now with these yer dunkeys. Much of the work be zimmiler zuch as driving tractor, hatten down dashels, bracken, regwort and all manner of blessed weeds about the vields, to mendin' busted vences and, would ee believe, "welding", of which I do the majority on account of 'aving the knack so-to-say. Finally, I gives the old varryer an 'and every Monday, so I s'pose you might say I've ended up looking at the backend of dunkeys!'

Malcolm Salter, Foreman, Brookfield Farm

'Being a part-time groom at Paccombe to 400 or so donkeys provides plenty of opportunity for "good conversation" with the donkeys who are, in the main, good listeners. The majority are so eager for individual attention that they almost queue up to be brushed. They seem reassured by the droning human voice; poetry has its place: "The coward dies a thousand deaths, the brave man only one . . ." can be quoted, in the right tones, to calm an apprehensive donkey! In summer, when they're shedding coats by the sack-load, they gather round you in groups, impatient to be brushed clear of matted coat, mud and flies. Those who know you come up and point out with their noses which bit of anatomy needs attention! Foals lay on entertainment, either by cavorting and wrestling with each other, or with you and your equipment. It's never dull! The chief delight, however, is wooing the newer, very timid ones, persuading them to risk contact with people and encouraging the more pessimistic donkeys to show an interest in life. It's very rewarding when, in response to your calling his name, a sad dilapidated-looking donkey at last raises his head with interest.' *Deirdre Golden, Part-time Groom, Paccombe Farm*

'I am Head Groom and care for the new arrivals at the Sanctuary. These donkeys stay with us for several weeks to make sure they have no infections, have full medical checks carried out and have time to settle in to a new way of life. They are often rather bewildered and nervous at the change of surroundings and need a lot of care, extra feeding and fuss to help them settle down.'

Gill Pudenz, Head Groom, Isolation Department

> 'My job as a groom down on the farm
> Is to see the donkeys come to no harm
> When they are ill with medicines we heal
> If they are thin they get an extra meal
> Their coats we brush to keep them nice and clean
> Then they roll in the earth, "typical", know what I mean?
> With love and care our donkeys enjoy life
> Just peace and tranquillity, no trouble or strife.'
>
> *Sue Walker, Farm Worker/Groom, Paccombe Farm*

SLADE MAGIC

'I watched quietly last week, as one of our schools who cater for the most seriously handicapped children used the arena. Only three donkeys had been chosen for the session as the children were so handicapped. As the session ended Alfred and Wilma were taken out but Harry, a strong grey gelding, waited quietly in the arena, his volunteer handler just with a gentle hand on his neck. Then I heard it – yells and screams from the play room and a nine-year-old, deeply disturbed boy was helped by two teachers across the floor. Harry watched him, perfectly quiet, not moving an inch as the noise advanced towards him. Suddenly the flailing hands touched Harry. The silence was uncanny – suddenly the boy stopped shouting and quietly the riding staff lifted him onto the donkey's back. The boy is so handicapped that he cannot sit upright and when riding has to lean back on his hands, which are on the donkey's back. As he passed, quiet at last, his fingers were gently rubbing the donkey and for the first time he had a calm expression.

I am told by the hospital staff that the twenty-minute ride on Harry once a week is the only time that child is calm – quite an achievement for Harry!'

44

With Camera and Handbag

With their large wistful eyes, big ears and furry coats, donkeys can be most successful subjects to photograph. They have many endearing qualities, but they are also possessed of an overwhelming curiosity and seem to be attracted to cameras like iron filings to a magnet. This can be awkward if you have your eye on a good shot only to see through the lens the star of your picture advancing steadily towards you, the head looming larger and larger, and it is only too easy in these circumstances to produce a rather distorted image as you can see in the picture of the grey donkey on p. 47.

Great patience is required on the part of the photographer and you must give the donkeys time to get used to you, even if it means sitting in a damp field for a couple of hours. The slide of the mare and foal is an example of patience rewarded. I waited ages for something interesting to happen; the first shot was hopeful, but the second one (shown here) was just what I wanted.

Donkeys come in different colours and sizes. The Poitou donkey from France, for example, is huge, dark brown and very hairy. It is important when photographing an animal like this to have a human in the picture to give an idea of the relative size.

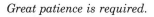

Great patience is required.

Our donkeys and mules at the Sanctuary spend the winter months in special quarters until the spring comes and the pastures have recovered. When they are first let out the donkeys are crazy with joy and really let rip – galloping madly around and performing quite amazing gymnastics. The photographer can get some great pictures, but you have to be quick on the draw! The trick is to get your camera moving at the same speed as the animal. To do this you must get your subject in focus in the lens, then sweep the camera round, keeping the subject in the centre of your lens all the time and in focus. Once you have got your camera moving, choose your moment and take the picture. It takes practice to get it right but is most rewarding when you do: the foal illustrated here was a typical example. Obviously, a fast film, that is a high ASA, 400 or more, is a good idea as you can keep your exposure very short.

A faster film and shorter exposure would have been better.

The angle and position from which you take your picture makes a great deal of difference. If you are photographing an animal using a fairly wide angle lens and are standing close to the animal, unless you squat down, the animal will appear to have very short legs and a large head.

Every photographer has his favourite equipment. I have two old and trusted Olympus cameras, an OM1N and OM2, and my most useful lens has turned out to be a Vivitar Series 1 28-105mm. When abroad, working in very bright sunlight, I like a polarizing filter. These days, however, there are so many excellent automatic and compact cameras that it is very easy to work out a combination to suit each individual.

I find working with a zoom lens especially fascinating. The 28-105mm is very useful, as I can use the 28mm facility for shots in tight corners, such as stables, and gradually increase the focal length to get candid shots of people and animals a little further off. It is, however, very easy to get a distorted picture with the wide angle lens, as I have already illustrated in the picture of the grey donkey with the over-large head. Equally, the wide angle is not good for distance shots of people or animals as they are much too small in relation to the rest of the picture.

My other useful lens is an Olympus 75-150mm. I suppose some people may regard the limit to 150mm as being a little too short and prefer the more usual 75-210mm but I like the Olympus optics. This lens is useful for more candid pictures of animals and people as you can be further away and, hopefully, they will not notice you. Donkeys take a great interest in handbags and I have managed to get some good pictures of them investigating the possessions of unsuspecting visitors (see p. 48). It is particularly useful for children who, although they invariably photograph delightfully, will, if they notice you, start to pose and look very self-conscious.

The 50mm lens, which is usually supplied as the basic lens with a 35mm camera, should not be too readily discarded in favour of other lenses. It is after all the lens which is closest to the normal human eye vision and certainly has its place in your camera equipment.

Choosing the right speed of film for the conditions in which you are working is very important. The ASA is the measure of the film speed. The lower the number of the ASA the finer the film grain. This is important in slide film, which is going to be projected as a much larger image, or is going to be published in an article or a book. It is also important in colour or black and white prints if they are going to be enlarged. The finer the grain the sharper the picture. A fast film, one with an ASA of 400 or even 1600, means that you can use a very short exposure time. This, in turn, means that there is less chance of movement of your subject or of camera wobble and it is also useful in low light conditions. However, the film emulsion of a fast film has different characteristics to that of slower film and tends to have a slightly grainy appearance when enlarged. You have to decide what speed of film best suits your purposes and it is fun to experiment with the different film speeds until you achieve a satisfying result.

Filters are another interesting aspect of photography and are fun to experiment with if you have the time. I find that in bright sunny conditions a yellow filter for black and white film certainly makes a more interesting picture. I have already mentioned the polarizing filter which I use for colour slides and prints. It seems to minimize glare and you get a beautifully deep, blue sky.

The head is out of proportion.

Light is one of the most important and tantalizing elements in photography. Early morning and early evening light can be extremely beautiful and produce very satisfying photographs. Also, on a really brilliant sunny day enticing your subject into a shady corner adjacent to a bright sunny spot can produce a beautiful luminescent effect.

Always have your flash with you. I have sometimes succumbed to leaving it behind and have usually regretted it. Apart from indoor shots, it is very useful to use as a fill-in if your subject is standing with his back to the light and cannot be manoeuvred into a more useful position.

I do not use a tripod on my trips abroad as I really cannot carry anything more and also the shots I take usually have to be pretty fast and generally there isn't time to set up a tripod. However, I do believe that, if possible, it is always better to use a tripod as the quality of the photographs is enormously improved in many cases.

Don't forget to insure your equipment, particularly when travelling abroad. A really good camera bag is a worthwhile investment and don't forget the little packets of silicon gel to put in with those expensive lenses to combat the changes in temperature and the resulting humidity.

June Evers

Donkeys also take a great interest in handbags!

48

The Trouble with Travel

You Are What You Eat

When working in Mexico three years ago we spent a great deal of time in a tiny village called Capula, miles from anywhere, where conditions were primitive. The donkeys were the main method of transport and had to carry water from a well some eight miles away. We were appalled at the conditions, not only for the donkeys, but also for the people and particularly for the children in the school that we visited. We always try to educate children on the needs of donkeys in foreign countries as frequently they are the ones who actually care for the donkey when it isn't working, and so we went to the tiny school to impress on the children how necessary it was to treat the donkeys well and look after them.

We were horrified at what we found: there were absolutely no materials for the children to use, no slates, no crayons, no paper – absolutely nothing – even to the extent of no desks and no chairs, and the children sat around in classrooms with sand on the floor and on this they drew and did their lessons. The fact that there was no water into the village was obviously an enormous deterrent to improving conditions and so we contacted the American Government as I felt they were the nearest neighbours and should be able to help. Senator Barry Goldwater wrote a nice reply to my request that they try to get water through to this village, and, very much to our joy and surprise, on our next visit some six months later, a water supply had been laid on! We took the opportunity to bring a vanload of equipment for the school which consisted of all sorts of teaching materials, books, crayons, and even cleaning equipment, buckets and mops and so on, as they were now able to improve their primitive washing and toilet facilities with the use of running water. They had the equivalent of what we would call a parent/teacher association and the parents were so delighted with the help we had given them that, poor as they were, they decided to lay on a special treat for us.

On this particular occasion I was accompanied by June Evers, Don Bliss (our American parasitologist), Dr Aline de Aluja from the Mexican Veterinary University, and the vet who we were training to work for us, Enrique Nunez. Somewhat to our horror we found ourselves invited to a luncheon in our honour; we are always rather wary of eating and drinking abroad. All sorts of diseases, to which our systems are totally unaccustomed, are present in both the drinking water and a lot of the food. However, there seemed no way out of this. Dr de Aluja told us that they had gone to great lengths and had all put up money that could be ill spared to provide a meal. We were shown into part of a small mill which had been converted for the day, the seats being sacks on which we sat, and

" I warned him about going around whistling Viva Espana!"

five planks laid across piles of sacks to form a table. Don Bliss, who
had vehemently declared that he could eat nothing that hadn't been
made in the hotel at which we were staying, had at first refused to
even sit down, despite pleading from Dr de Aluja who was very
afraid of upsetting the feelings of those who had sacrificed so much
to give us this meal. However, he caught sight of an unopened
bottle of whisky on the table and this seemed to persuade him to
join us in the repast.

I don't really know how to describe the food we were offered. It
was served in chipped enamel washing-up bowls and at first sight
appeared to be a peculiar brownish liquid on which lumps of fat
were bobbing and small bags were floating. Without any fuss a
large ladle of this was spooned into the bowls in front of us. June
and I looked round, hoping that somebody else would start to eat,
so that we could try and sort out what we were supposed to do, but
before we had time to give more than a cursory glance at the bowl

SOPHIE'S TRAVELLING CIRCUS

Twenty-one-year-old Crook student Sophie Thurnham set out to trace the footsteps of Hannibal who together with his army crossed the Alps by elephant. With donkey and collection of pets, Sophie is making progress on the same trail, and hoping to raise several thousands of pounds for MENCAP.

Her mother who is hoping to join her for a visit with her brother Stephen in August called in with a letter for us this week in which Sophie tells her own story:

I am writing from the tiny village of St Martin, buried in the French foothills of the Pyrenees. We are camped in a small field and I am recovering from the flu – I knew I wouldn't be able to last the whole trip without getting ill.

However, being grounded for a few days has given me a chance to do some much needed mending and washing, and to look back and write about the past 14 weeks since I sailed from Plymouth.

I have now walked about 1,000 km, through countryside more beautiful than I had dared hope for. I had never been to

mainland Spain before; discovering it was full of surprises.

Though I was often only 20 or 30 km from the sea, the land I have travelled through and the people I have met have seemed a million miles from the discos and the tower blocks of the costas. I have walked through vast mountains and wildernesses for up to three days without meeting a soul. Often in the small isolated villages, I am the first foreigner many of the older people have ever met, which I find very moving.

The friendliness and the generosity of the Spanish amazed me. Most of them thought I was completely mad – to walk anywhere other than out of sheer necessity is to a Spaniard incomprehensible. Yet they welcomed me into their homes in bad weather as if I were a relative, and were very interested in everything about me – what I am doing, where I come from, and what I think of their country. The old peasant way of life is still living in many parts of Spain; almost every day we meet shepherds and goatherds leading their flocks over the hills, and in the south horses and

donkeys are still used in the fields.

My Spanish donkey was wonderful, and it was a very sad day when I had to part with her before entering France. I named her Hasdrubella (Bella for short) after the Carthaginian leader before Hannibal. She was light brown, very small and very naughty. She ate my entire food supply more times

in front, some bright yellow saffron rice was ladled on top and rapidly sank into the brown liquid. It was at this stage we realized that we were the only ones who were being asked to eat; everybody else was standing back looking, and Dr de Aluja immediately took a large mouthful and then proceeded to pick out one of the little bags half submerged in the bowl. She carefully undid this and out of it took a small piece of gristly chicken. The bags were in fact made of the outer skin of the cactus leaf; the chicken had apparently been ceremoniously killed and was regarded as the *pièce de resistance* for our feast. We never really identified other objects floating in our bowls; suffice it to say that

than I care to remember, and at night I was forced to tether her, not because she would wander off, but because she tried to get inside the tent with me. Although very quaint in theory, this habit was not very endearing when my tent fell down at 3 a.m. She was a wonderful plodder, very slow (we averaged less than two miles an hour), but very steady, and

after three months she had become a very good friend. I luckily managed to find a good home for her – a family who wanted her for their children to ride.

I crossed the border by train, and scoured the French countryside for another donkey – not an easy task as they seem to be a rarity this side of the Pyrenees. Eventually I found Hannibal – he is a Poitou donkey, very big and strong, with long shaggy dark brown hair, and an extremely friendly temperament.

We had only been going a few days before I got struck down by flu, but so far, so good. He walks much faster than Bella, but gets tired more easily, so our mileage seems to work out about the same. He is wonderful with children, so hopefully will make a good ride for Stephen when he joins us in August.

My confidence as a young woman travelling alone has grown steadily; it has been a question of using my head and always putting safety first. After an encounter with horse thieves in the first week, during which my little mongrel George proved utterly useless as a guard dog, I bought a Dobermann who sits outside my tent

at night, ears pricked. I camp either in the middle of nowhere, miles along a little-used path, or else next to a house or farm, where I know I can get help should I need it.

Bogus, my Dobermann, had a surprise in store for me. On May 8 – six weeks after I bought her, as we were crossing a huge iron bridge over the River Ebro, she gave birth. So we now resemble something of a travelling animal circus. Dido and Cleopatra, two rapidly growing very beautiful puppies, now travel in a sling over my shoulder. I shall have to find homes for them soon, but in the meantime, they are a constant source of amusement – I never have a bored moment.

After three and a half months, I have become totally addicted to the travelling life, and find it very hard to imagine 'normal' life in England. I look (and smell I fear) like a very seasoned gypsy. I'm ridiculously fit and healthy, browner than I've ever been and my hair is so bleached it will soon be white. The Alps are now beckoning; so beware Rome, the second Hannibal and his army are fast approaching.

From *Westmoreland Gazette*, July 14th, 1989

fortunately the taste of curry seemed to conceal the other rather obnoxious tastes that one suddenly became aware of.

Don Bliss managed one teaspoonful and then said he wasn't feeling very well, and sat hopefully waiting for the bottle of whisky to be opened. This, however, was not to be; it was decoration, having been obtained by the head of the village on a trip some years before, and apparently was ceremoniously produced at any major function, although never opened. We were all, however, treated to glasses of pulka. This innocuous-looking, milky liquid, occasionally mistaken for skimmed milk at first sight, was once again produced from the cactus plant and had quite a dramatic effect on us all, in particular on Don Bliss, who hadn't been able to eat anything to absorb the very high alcohol level.

One of the biggest problems abroad is having to eat food for which you know that your stomach is neither prepared nor accustomed. I was taken to see where they had cooked the food later and, having watched what they did, I can now give you the recipe for this feast and the methods of cooking it.

1. Collect small twigs and pieces of wood, and add to the top four dried pats of donkey dung. These will ensure that the cooking is long and slow, and this use of donkey dung, flattened and dried, is prevalent throughout many parts of Mexico and Africa. The large cooking pot, which is slung over the fire, held by a tripod arrangement of sticks, should not have been washed, as it should retain flavours from previous cookings.

2. Catch the chicken to be prepared for the meal, and having despatched it, use every single piece of the bone and flesh in the pot.

3. The water is used from the well (unless you have a supply which is nearer to hand), and does not necessarily need to be clean as you will in fact be boiling it.

4. Place all the bits of the chicken, including the entrails, into the water and cover, boiling as long as the wood and the donkey dung last.

5. Find a large cactus plant, take the outside leaves and, as they dry, strip off the surface which can be used as wrapping material. Once the stew has cooled, take out the pieces of chicken and by hand wrap them in the cactus leaves. Pop all these back into the pot, and this is then ready to serve when required. *Bon appetit!*

In Tunisia, where we were helping donkeys in a remote area called Tozeur, we were once again enveigled into eating with a family, despite our protests, and this also turned out to be quite a dramatic affair.

The main meal appeared to be a type of couscous, and again the method of cooking was primitive to say the least. The water in this case was drawn from a small well in the middle of the family's courtyard. The old dirty plastic bucket which was used to draw the water was not an encouraging sign and, although we weren't allowed to see the actual preparation of the couscous, I found some very strange things indeed on the dishes placed before us. We were quite able to accept the couscous itself as the main basic ingredient, although this had been cooked to such a state that it was almost a total grey mush. Into this had been put various small pieces of chicken and unidentifiable entrails which gave the whole

Eieio

The Borders has echoed with sounds o'er the years
The tramping of feet and of laughter and tears
From the whaup on the moorland to sheep on the hills
But a new sound at last our Borderland fills.
For Kearney has gathered six sheep with brown marks
The air's filled with baaing but as yet there's no barks
He's shouting 'come in bye', 'get oot bye' and 'stay'
Yes, you've guessed who is rounding up sheep that
   will stray.
The wife's oot o' breath and the kids do get mad
At the orders and signals sent oot by their dad.
We run here and there, we shout and we wave
Shed **these** six sheep is the order **HE** gave.
At the end of the day he won't give a cuss
At who is most puggled – whether it's them or us!

DON'T ever think he's finished at that.
He thinks he is Noah filling his ark.
He sits and he plans about ducks, geese and hens,
Angora goats filling hundreds of pens.
But that's all in the future, he's got other schemes
That have come to fruition – they're no longer dreams.
Two ghostly white donkeys have now made their home
With the sheep and the kids – no more will they roam.
They're called Dylan and Kia – they're both lovely boys
And the neighbours excuse their terrible noise.
They're in in the evening and out in the day
They never stop feeding on sheep nuts or hay
He tends them like weans but you really should know
The air's rent with orders of 'walk on' and 'whoa'

There's only one problem with this pastoral scene
THEY haven't quite grasped what these orders mean.
They both seem so clever – they watch what he says
But pay no attention and go their own ways
When he orders 'walk on' they come to a halt.
The words are quite simple – so **who** is at fault.
Perhaps they are Gaelic, or German or Dutch
They're definitely not Scottish we now know that much!
But they'll learn by example – so out with the reins
Plus a bright scarlet halter – we call out their names.
'Now stand at the railing and see how it's done'
– Put the halter on, Danny, and just watch **HIM** run!
At the end of the day though I guess we'll forget
The cultural diff'rence and treat them as pets!

But the pantomime's on almost every night.
He's heaving and shoving and pushing all right.
He's coaxing with titbits and just now and then
They both do things perfect but won't do it again
He plans that he'll train them to trot with the cart
But their last destination could be Newtown mart!
I have to admit though they're both lovely boys
And we're far away so we don't hear the noise.
They're lovely and friendly and seem to enjoy
The care and attention they get from our boy!
He's full of ideas for hobbies – I'll bet
We fully agree it's the best he's had yet!

Mrs V. Kearney

thing the most peculiar flavour. I was trying to eat mine when I suddenly realized I had something round and chewy in my mouth that was almost impossible to swallow, and, turning my head slightly, I managed to eject it. There, sitting in my hand, looking at me, was the eye of either a sheep or a goat! I was absolutely horrified, and had to put it in my pocket, as I couldn't possibly swallow it, and tried to look across to June to warn her of what she was going to find if she wasn't very lucky. To my horror, our host, who was picking into his couscous, suddenly found the other eye and, as is the custom in these countries where one gives the special delicacies to one's guest, before I had time to stop him he had reached across and pushed it in my mouth! How I managed a polite nod of thanks whilst desperately trying to work out a way of getting rid of my problem, I shall never know, but I can no longer

COMMUNITY SNARED IN A TRAP OF OWN MAKING

The village was caught in a trap of its own making. Men engaged in fierce arguments, women threw accusations at each other: should they have disposed of their mules so rashly? Now they were at the mercy of muleteers from other villages. Bhagwa, one of the most hard-working women in the village, was running down the hill, screaming: 'I'll nab him first. Don't any of you dare try.' Rushing after her, Durgu the blacksmith roared: 'What's she mean he's hers? A muleteer serves whoever pays him.'

Several men conferring earnestly in the temple square broke off as Bhagwa and Durgu walked back, still bickering. 'You've got a wife, son, and brother to do your carrying, you scoundrel,' Bhagwa fumed. 'I have no one. I need the mules to get the manure to

the field.' Durgu appealed to the men in the square: 'It wasn't unfair of me to try to get in first, was it?'

'Stop your fighting and save your strength, you'll be needing it soon,' Daultoo the muleteer called out jauntily as he strode into view following three mules laden with sacks of grain. Catching sight of us, he spat out the tobacco he was chewing and winked. 'Watch them fight when the potato season starts. They foolishly sold their mules and now they're trapped,' he said as he walked past, on the way to his own village, ignoring the villagers who were importuning him for his mules' services.

The village was indeed caught between the devil and the deep sea. For generations mules had carried heavy loads in these rugged mountains,

transporting manure to the terraced fields, stone and slate for the huts. At harvest time, they occasionally took grain from fields high on the hillside to watermills down in the valley. Sometimes, people who couldn't afford a horse hired a mule to go to a distant village.

When the potatoes – the village's main cash crop – were ready, even a rich villager who might own a horse had to depend on mules. It was the potato season that made them economically viable. All day for more than a month mules would carry sacks, each containing a 100 kg of potatoes, across the fields; then ford the river, climb up the rocky muletrack, and deposit the sacks on the road leading to town, to be picked up by buses or trucks.

But when the new road to the village was built and a bus ser-

eat oysters, as just the feeling of the oyster in my mouth reminds me of that meal, and the horrors of accepting our host's hospitality.

My colleague June Evers and I had another memorable meal while we were working in Egypt alongside the Brooke Hospital. June, who was the Chief Superintendent of Radiography at Wonford Hospital in Exeter, was working there with an Egyptian doctor who, knowing that she was travelling to Cairo, suggested that perhaps she would take out some parcels for his family there. During our stay we were invited to a meal at their home, which seemed a nice thought, as the accommodation at the Hotel Horace was indeed very poor; the rooms were dirty and there was a large number of fleas and nasty flying insects which seemed to have made our room their particular venue. We were delighted, therefore, to be invited and although surprised that they weren't going to pick us up until 10 o'clock in the evening, felt that our stomachs could in fact hold on until this time for possibly our first good meal since arriving in Cairo. However, it wasn't to be served so soon. We were engaged in pleasant conversation for over one vice promised, mule owners had cause for worry. Now the bus would collect the village produce; the mules, instead of carrying burdens, would become a burden themselves. A mule could earn 30 rupees for a day's hire, but it needed 25 rupees' worth of feed daily.

If, with the opening of the road, demand for their services fell, no one would be able to afford the luxury of 'guest-feeding' unemployed mules. They must get rid of them without delay, though a forced sale would mean far less money than the 8,000 rupees (£340) or so a mule cost. And forced sales they all proved to be. When the bus finally arrived and replaced the mules, the owners congratulated themselves: the loss would have been greater if they had waited for a better price.

But when the village, in its collective wisdom, decided that the bus service did more harm than good, and brought about its termination, the mule owners knew they had made a serious mistake. The potato harvest was due soon. The rich and the outside traders would be able to hire a truck to the village. For the poor the price would be too high. With mules, they could have taken their potatoes to the main road to be loaded, as in the past, on buses whose rates were cheaper.

The difference might be only a few rupees a sack; but for some families this could add up to the difference between having enough food for many months or for just a few. As always, the poor would be hit the hardest.

The mules' former owners tried desperately to buy them back from other villagers. But word of their predicament had spread. Not a single mule was to be had in the whole area for less than 12,000 rupees (nearly £500).

The villagers are now seething with rage, blaming one another. 'We don't have the money to pay an extra 4,000 rupees,' they tell us. 'Even if we did, we'd much rather buy food or a buffalo than pay blackmail rates.'

The canny muleteers who are demanding nothing less than 12,000 know that a remote mountain village, without assured road transport, cannot function indefinitely without mules. Yet the villagers will not, they swear, buy a mule at 12,000 rupees. And the mule owners have sworn not to sell for less.

The hopes of many a poor household which looked forward to a potato income to see it through the year now hang in the balance.

From *The Times*,
September 10th, 1988
© *Victor Zorza & Veenu Sandal, 1988*

and a half hours, during which time an assortment of drinks was served. Our stomachs were rumbling quite noticeably by the time dinner was served at around 11.30 p.m.

The meal began with a series of three starters consisting of a strange pâté the origin of which was obscure, an extremely thick soup of vegetables and unknown objects, and then an unfamiliar piece of fruit which was very acidic. Following this came three large plates, one of which contained portions of rabbit, a selection of chicken joints and a large roast of beef, all cooked so well that it was almost impossible to get a knife into any of the flesh. Our host immediately piled our plates full of all three types of meat and sat back to watch us. It is so difficult in Egypt, where manners seem to dictate that only the guests eat whilst the hosts sit and watch, and although we had been extremely hungry before the meal started, our overladen plates suddenly became an almost impossible hurdle. June must have one of the best stomachs I've ever known when travelling abroad; she quite definitely puts this down to having had to eat hospital food for so many years; whatever the reason, she certainly has built up an enormous

CLOVELLY'S DONKEY POST COMES TO END

Clovelly's famous donkey post – unique in this country – officially ended in March 1964. But Peter and Paul, the donkeys 70-year-old Mr Cecil Braund had been using for the mail delivery for the 14 years he has been doing the job, will not be going into retirement.

No longer will Peter and Paul have any mail to carry, but they will be continuing with their normal summer-time practice of giving rides to children and posing against the picturesque back-ground.

The delivery of the mail by donkey to the post office situated half way down the steep cobbled High-street and the return journey to the top of the hill where the mail van waited, has been going on at Clovelly for a good many years. Long ago the donkeys were kept quite busy, and at Christmas time, in particular, they were both often fully loaded for the trip up and down, but recently business has been falling off, and for the past 18 months or so the donkeys have been working on a casual basis.

'There just isn't the amount of parcels and that to be carried nowadays,' said Mr Braund yesterday. 'It's a sad job really after all these years, but I suppose it's a sign of the times.'

From *Western Morning News*, April 1st, 1964

tolerance to food bugs and infections. My stomach, however, is slightly more sensitive and I knew after three mouthfuls of the stringy rabbit that I was in for a tough time! As soon as we seemed to clear one part of the plate our host would lean across with another slice of beef or another rabbit leg or another piece of chicken, and the same task lay ahead of us yet again. It took almost an hour to get to the point where they realized that we couldn't manage any more, and we were relieved when the staff came in and took away the plates. June and I managed a sickly smile at each other, and looked forward to a cup of coffee. To our absolute amazement and horror, in came two large steaming tureens. These were full of a special type of Nile perch, a local delicacy, and one of which, of course, we had to partake to keep our over-enthusiastic host happy. Two or three large perch were served onto our plates before we had time to make any comment, and then, and only then, did they bring in gigantic plates of vegetables; large husks of sweetcorn, potatoes and a strange mixture that looked like mashed swede and turnip (but wasn't), all covered in a thick white sauce. I won't bore you with the details of how we tried to get through this next course but I'm sure you will understand that when they brought in the steamed puddings and the enormous cream and chocolate gateau . . .

Tanzanian Breakfast

We were called to Tanzania by Mr R. Fischer of the Tanga Integrated Rural Development Programme to advise on their Draught Animal Project. The team selected to train farmers how to plough had very little experience with donkeys. The whole project was further complicated by the fact that the wherewithal to purchase the donkeys to be used in the ploughing scheme was not to be straight cash, but bicycles imported from Germany. On receiving their first bicycles the team exchanged these for donkeys and one of my first jobs on arrival was to look at the donkeys that they had purchased. To my horror I found a large number were very elderly and the first day of our visit was spent showing the very enthusiastic team how to age donkeys!

We had travelled from Tanga to Korogwe in central Tanzania, where the project was underway and, somewhat to our consternation, we found there were no hotels or accommodation in the area, with the exception of a very kind offer from Mr Fischer to share his house. He told us that his wife had originally intended to move with him to Korogwe with their children but had taken one look at the house and the area, and decided she would prefer to live in Tanga, where Mr Fischer retreated happily each weekend. For this reason they had not bothered to furnish their house in

East African donkey at rest.

Korogwe beyond the basic necessities and Mr Fischer had so many friends in the area that he didn't need to keep supplies of food in, as he was invited out each night for his evening meal. Luckily we were included in these splendid repasts. However, breakfast was a different matter and on our first morning we joined Mr Fischer in the garden for breakfast, which consisted of bread, honey and gallons of wonderful strong Tanzanian coffee. Both June and I are very fond of honey but we had not grasped the fact that Mr Fischer was engaged in a second project, this one not connected in any way with donkeys. He was trying to produce honey from African killer bees.

Not only the garden, where we sat for breakfast, but also the area where we worked later in the day where the donkeys were kept had what he called 'catchment boxes'. He lured the killer bees into the 'catchment boxes' and tried to persuade them to produce honey for his own consumption. Blissfully unaware of this we ladled oodles of honey onto our bread and began to enjoy our first meal in Korogwe. Within seconds we were surrounded by a swarm of killer bees, who seemed highly conscious that their efforts were being consumed before their very eyes! Despite Mr Fischer's repeated requests just to sit quietly as they wouldn't harm us, June and I wasted no time in beating a hasty retreat back into the house.

Our mission in Tanzania became even more difficult and dangerous than usual; little comments such as, 'I don't think you should stand there to give your lecture, Mrs Svendsen, because one of my catchment areas is immediately above where you are standing,' tended to make the whole project much livelier.

That was certainly one breakfast neither June nor I will ever forget.

If You Want to Get Ahead Get a Hat

We have just returned from a trip to Nigeria; we were invited there by the Veterinary Council of Nigeria, specifically by Dr Onoviran, who had previously visited the Sanctuary on a trip to the United Kingdom. The idea of the trip was to assess the necessity for help in Nigeria by visiting donkey markets throughout the country and to talk to the various Heads of Departments, to see what aid could be provided for the donkeys.

On arrival in Lagos we were met by Dr Onoviran and his colleagues. We were given a beautiful welcome by a group of about twenty children who were members of the Nigerian Society for the

Prevention of Cruelty to Animals. They not only presented my colleague, June Evers, and me with flowers, but they chanted their special oath of allegiance to protect and help all animals and then sang the most delightful little song, all in the confines of Lagos airport. Dr Onoviran had spent a lot of time talking to various people and had managed to form a little group called the Nigerian Donkey Protection Trust, and it was to this trust that I gave my first talk on our night of arrival. A rather special dinner was laid on and 24 VIPs and local dignitaries turned up with their wives who were most beautifully dressed in traditional costumes.

The following morning we were off at the crack of dawn to fly up to Abuja which is situated in approximately the centre of Nigeria. We spent the next seven days in the Veterinary Officer's car travelling steadily north looking at donkey markets, visiting District Agricultural Offices and Veterinary Offices en route, but meeting very, very few donkeys. We almost lost heart in an area called Bauchi as we were told there were many donkeys there but, despite travelling over 400 kilometres, we found only seven. The bad news then started coming through to us, that because of rinderpest, and other contagious diseases in both cattle and poultry, food was becoming short in Southern Nigeria and large numbers of donkeys were being shipped south for meat consumption. Apart from our worry and concern over the donkeys we began to feel physically weak, as not only was most of the food we were offered inedible but the water supplies began to run out and the local water was totally unacceptable to British stomachs!

Each area in Nigeria has its own Emir (the equivalent of royalty for the area) and we were invited to visit the Emir of Keffi. We hadn't realized how important these people were until we were ushered into the large house which was used as the Royal Headquarters. Dr Onoviran had warned us that we should be prepared to curtsey and to call the Emir 'Your Highness' but we weren't prepared for the scribes sitting down the side of the room, the presence of the important elders of the village and the bodyguards dressed in brilliant red, green and yellow long-flowing robes. June and I were accompanied by Dr Onoviran, his veterinary surgeon colleagues, the Keffi Chief Veterinary Officer and the Agricultural Officers. We were seated on large chairs which were placed down the left-hand side of the room from the Emir. Each of our party made a speech in turn and then I was asked to speak. I was able to point out how we hoped to be able to help the Nigerians by improving the health and working capacity of their donkeys and thereby extending the donkeys' life-span. The Emir then asked me to step forward as he wished to make a presentation and, completely unsuspecting, I stood in front of him wondering what was coming next. A large leather and straw hat was passed to the Emir who, with great ceremony, placed it on my head. I realized this was a moment of great seriousness and importance, and I was, indeed, very honoured; unfortunately the honour had not been bestowed on women before, and in particular on English women! The fact of the matter was that men have larger heads than women, and in Nigeria the head to be crowned would normally be wearing a turban, so you can imagine what happened; one moment I was looking at the Emir and the next, my vision was completely obliterated and I could feel the hat resting firmly on my nose! There was a moment of embarrassed silence until I realized what a spectacle I must be making of myself. I gave a desperate look at June, who was convulsed with laughter, and then at the veterinary surgeons who were equally amused and, finally, lifting my head back so that I could see the Emir from under the brim of the hat, I burst out laughing myself. To my great joy his face broke into a big smile and he had to sit down as he was laughing so much. Obviously we weren't allowed to take a photograph at the time but this photograph taken in Zaria shortly afterwards gives you some idea of what I looked like!

In the hat!

'ZONKEY' FROM ZIMBABWE

In 1981 peasant farmer Clemence Mushonga (33) placed one of his female donkeys in a paddock with some tame zebras ... and the result is – an animal Mushonga calls a 'Zonkey'.

The 'Zonkey' called Stompie now aids three donkeys tilling Mushonga's fields, 46 kms from the town of Battlefields, south west of Harare in Zimbabwe.

'He is a bit stronger than the donkeys,' said Mushonga, who is planting corn this year, 'but he acts on all the commands like they do.'

From *Greenock Telegraph*, March 1986

Eventually we arrived at Kano and, although by this time we were extremely weak from lack of food and water, for the first time my heart really lifted. We began to see donkeys in very large numbers and, having found a Chinese restaurant and eaten them out of rice, our strength returned and we were able to start treating donkeys in the markets, realizing the aim of our trip. There was, however, one last official task; on our very last morning, when we were due to be at the airport at 11 a.m., we were told that first I was to meet the Director General of Veterinary Services for Northern Nigeria and from there we were to be escorted to the Emir's palace in Kano where we were to be officially received. Having met one Emir I was rather concerned that I might be offered yet another hat.

I gave a talk to approximately twenty visiting vets at the Veterinary Director's office and we all went in a procession of cars to the Emir's palace. This really was a palace; it was enormous and the whole place was crowded with people. We were ushered with great ceremony into a beautiful room that had the most ornate ceiling. Apparently Prince Philip had been the previous guest officially welcomed by the Emir and I'm sure he must have been as impressed as we were. After a few moments' wait we heard a strange chanting and singing outside which indicated that the Emir was being escorted to his Throne Room. We were then organized to form a procession and led up a long passageway, lined on each side by guards, to the Throne Room. This absolutely magnificent room had two thrones facing us and a long low couch on which the Emir was sat. The Director of Veterinary Services and I were at the head of the procession, June and Dr Onoviran were behind and the others followed. I walked forward towards the Emir and suddenly realized that, with the exception of June, everybody else was on all fours! We progressed rather awkwardly and slowly up to the feet of the Emir and I managed to curtsey, although not very elegantly, as I was wearing trousers! The Emir, of course, had to be addressed as 'Your Royal Highness' and I felt quite moved as he took my hand and welcomed me. The official speeches then took place. The Emir speaks perfect English and understood my speech but he replied in his local language through an interpreter. We were received for over twenty minutes and were very impressed by the welcome we were given. The Emir was extremely interested in our work and the help we were giving to his people and, at the end of the audience, he expressed a wish that he could

THE DISPLACED BEASTS OF THE WEST

The comparative peace of a highway that goes nowhere (except, at length, to the sea) solicits the more natural kinds of transport. I hope the kids from round the hill will remember how it feels to double up on the back of their father's big draught mare, and to urge her into a canter on the way home from the outfield. I hope my neighbour at the bend will ride his jennet on the road for another 20 years, if jennets live that long.

'Jennet', says the dictionary: 'A small Spanish horse.' But the Irish countryman, taking up a word, bestows it where he chooses. The jennet is really a hinny, a cross got by a stallion on a female donkey. Not to be confused with the mule, which is got by a jackass on a mare. But in some parts, mules and hinnies alike have been called 'jennets', so we are not much further on.

'Should they not have the best of both worlds?' asks Paul Muldoon in his poem about mules. They were certainly prized by the western smallholder: so much muscle with such modest appetite. The hinny, on the other hand, inherits a neigh instead of a bray, but lacks the mule's size and stamina.

The donkey's bray – that raucous two-tone blast which can make a beast fart with the effort – evolved for seeking company across the wide deserts of Nubia; the long ears, for picking up the echo at great distance. Logically, there should be more braying in the west of Ireland these days, as the donkey population thins out so dramatically. In fact there seems less – as if the asses think they might last longer by keeping quiet.

The ass is so at home in the western landscape, so much a part of its romantic iconography of whitewashed cottage, turf fire, rosy-cheeked children loading *cliabhs* on the bog, that it seems timeless in its belonging. In fact, to go by the research of Professor Mahaffy 'On the Introduction of the Ass as a Beast of Burden into Ireland', the donkey was spreading here only at the time Wellington was fighting the peninsula wars at the beginning of the nineteenth century.

It came in to replace the horses which were being shipped off to the British cavalry in Spain. The north-east counties got donkeys first, from Scotland, but the animals failed to thrive in the northern cold: the west suited them far better. How odd, as Estyn Evans has said, that a region which could use the donkey so well and had such ancient links with Iberia, should ultimately acquire it through Ireland's back door in Ulster.

By the end of the century, there were some 200,000 donkeys working on Ireland's farms. Hundreds more, in long strings, trotted ahead of the drovers on the roads to the east coast ports. Shipped to Wales, they set off on foot again, many to end up in the weekly market at Islington, which sold 3,000 donkeys a year.

One export trade in Irish donkeys these days is swifter and more discreet. It leads back, ironically, through the North to Scotland, to a factory making pet-food.

The donkey's sudden redundancy is due mainly, of course, to the arrival of the 'sausage machine' – the tractor-driven turf-cutter, operated by contractor, which now churns out turf in bulk on hillsides throughout the west. Spread automatically and quick to dry, the sods need only to be gathered and taken home. Gone, in many places, are the family turf-banks, their keshes bridged with bog-deal; gone, therefore, the need for the sure-footed tireless ass and its balanced pair of panniers.

As the *slean* gathers rust in the barn, and the woodworm claims straddle and *cliabhs*, more and more donkeys are being turned out to graze 'the long acre' of the wayside – and never brought back in. Asses are companionable, they team up in pairs and half-dozens, perhaps visit the Donkey Sanctuary at some time in the future. He allowed a photograph to be taken (a rare honour) outside the Throne Room and we were then whisked away to the airport, just in time to catch our flight.

On the plane I deliberated how to teach our staff to chant the welcoming words we had heard in Kano and how to crawl on all fours!

even 15 at a time. After months, perhaps, of straying back and forth between villages, one gets hit by a car or somebody complains to the guards.

And the guards, these days, are very pleased to pass the problem on to the growing network of people who will collect straying or unwanted donkeys and give them sanctuary, safe employment, or a peaceful old age. At the centre of this network is the Irish Donkey Sanctuary at Liscarroll, near Mallow in County Cork, which is the offshoot of a busy donkey welfare organisation in England. Since it opened in August, 1987, Liscarroll has taken in 435 donkeys – more than 100 of them since the beginning of this year.

At the sanctuary, the donkeys are wormed and vaccinated and have their 'Turkish slippers' trimmed back into proper hooves. Then they are

found a home: an acre of grass, at least, for a donkey – perhaps even for two, since donkeys form extraordinarily close attachments in a herd, nothing to do with sex, and Liscarroll will not split a pair of friends. I like that. They also send out an inspector to the billet. At the same time, they won't leave people stuck with veterinary bills, and they'll take the donkey back if circumstances change: all very down to earth.

So – is the Irish rural donkey a threatened species, really? It has certainly been drastically 'marginalized' by the loss of its job on the bog. There is no incentive to breed new foals, though some will happen anyway.

But the donkey remains a serious and trouble-free draught animal for pulling a cart with small loads – the can of milk, plus stubble-chinned farmer, to the creamery, or a

pile of seaweed from the shore. As old men grow older, and such modest occupations are extinguished, it should not be hard to shape new ones in the make-believe world of tourism. Tourists like donkeys: they expect them in the Irish landscape, they provide lovely photo-opportunities – why not find ways of obliging? But donkeys employed just for beach rides and races? Perhaps not; that way lies abuse.

In the east, of course, the donkey is flourishing, if only to keep Jacintha's pony company in the paddock. Clipped and cared for, it is a very different animal (yet not really) from the dusty, disdained and now displaced beast of the west. To see donkeys as they might be, visit next month's Dublin Horse Show on its last day.

The mechanization of local turf-cutting was inevitable and overdue. For all that we romanticize the days on the bog, a lot of them were mere drudgery. What I do regret is the banishing of the donkey from the summer lives of country children. It is bad enough to see their fathers herding sheep or cattle from the seat of a car, but this loss of an animal's company, of responsibility for it, is another sad distancing from nature.

Michael Viney
from *Irish Times*,
June 9th, 1990

Language Problems

During the course of our work on behalf of donkeys round the world, we visit so many countries that, even if we had the ability, it would be almost impossible to learn every language. This can cause some problems.

The flights to and from Ethiopia are extremely exhausting and the entry formalities when we have arrived at the airport take a long time, especially as we are carrying veterinary supplies to treat donkeys. On one visit we were relieved to have got through by 7 a.m., after two hours of hassling with customs and immigration departments, and to be able to change into some clean clothes. In Ethiopia the hotel in Addis Ababa is the only place where we can be sure of getting water and this gives us the chance to clean up and get ready for the days ahead. Whilst getting ready June had washed her underwear and hung it out over the balcony. Having returned from a most successful visit to the British Ambassador, we were horrified to find that her knickers had vanished from the balcony. Peering over the ledge we saw that they had fallen down behind a very high wall and appeared totally inaccessible.

We sought out the only receptionist who understood any English. As we stood in the hotel foyer, we were definitely the main focus of interest. I carefully and slowly explained that my friend's knickers had fallen off the balcony and were down below our room in the enclosure.

'What is fallen? Please tell me . . .'

By this time I had run through the gamut of 'pants', 'underclothes' and 'knickers' but I did a little mimicry of trying to pull knickers on and take knickers off!

'Ah', she said, smiling. 'Now I understand.'

We both smiled at each other.

'So, please, will somebody find them and bring them up to our room?'

Her reply was not what we expected, and left us completely flattened. 'Yes, I will replace the shower curtain immediately!'

Vicious Donkeys

Every two years the World Association for the Advancement of Veterinary Parasitology holds its Congress and I have been privileged to be able to present a paper at each Congress I have been able to attend. The first was in Rio de Janeiro, followed by Montreal two years later, and in August 1989 the Congress was held in East Berlin, just three months before the wall came down.

As you may be aware, we have been interested in a very endangered species of donkey, the Poitou. This is the most beautiful donkey imaginable, standing over fourteen hands high, with a lovely long shaggy coat which at times hangs right down to the ground! There are only approximately eighty of these animals left in the world and I had been advised that there were three in the East Berlin Zoo.

I managed to ring the director of the zoo and was invited out to see the Poitou donkeys on the Friday afternoon of the Congress. Accompanied by Bill Jordan and Dr Aline de Aluja, who were also attending the Congress, we were taken by the director to the donkeys' enclosure. I was quite appalled to see the donkeys kept in what appeared to be a lion's cage. It was very heavily guarded

The 'vicious' donkey with anxious staff watching.

MAKING AN ASS OF THE LAW

No hill-farming family in the remotest upland fastness of Wales lives so securely in the old Celtic twilight as the Arran Islanders, off the west of Ireland, are considered to do by Irish mainlanders. And the regular influx of American tourists, alerted to the spartan, poetic life of the islanders by the plays of J. M. Synge, go back annually to their homes in the Middle West, happy in the stark awareness that they have visited a different world.

Yet even the Arran people draw the line at certain breaches of the modern code of civilized behaviour. A gang of 'lazy, shiftless, useless, crafty robbers' – having long lived rough on Inishmore, thieving and vandalizing, preying indiscriminately on natives and tourists – have at last been deported to the mainland by District Justice Mr Al O'Dea, with the stern valediction that they shall never set foot on the island again.

The eight dangerous dropouts were stray donkeys. They would steal your wallet or handbag if it was unguarded, but your cottage or caravan was fairer game if any potatoes were seen to be lying about it. In defence of the extreme penalty laid on the animals, Inishmore's resident policeman Garda Sean McDonagh has said: 'We had to take firm action. The law was made to look an ass.' It was, so.

These four-footed playboys of the western world may now console themselves with the thought that the island life never really suited them anyway. Since their migration, they have already found themselves honest jobs of donkey-work, as farm labourers in County Galway. But they have learned the chastening truth of the old Celtic saying: A marauding donkey will invade the very noose itself before she'll have enough of the pillaging.

From *Western Mail*,
April 4th, 1986

with great iron gates and when I suggested to the director that I would go in and talk to the donkeys, he was absolutely horrified, and advised me that it wasn't safe to enter as the donkeys were very vicious. I just couldn't believe this of the Poitou, who are a particularly soft and gentle breed of donkey, and so I insisted on being allowed in. I was amused when they hastily closed and bolted the gates behind me. However, as always with Poitou donkeys, they were absolutely beautiful. I approached them very quietly and slightly from the side; the donkeys' vision is such that it can't see straight ahead and I think the reason many people encounter problems with donkeys and find them difficult is because they will approach from directly in front of the animal and, as the donkey can't see exactly what is approaching, it obviously becomes concerned. I quietly went up to the donkeys, talking as I went, and within moments I was able to put my arm around them and start stroking them inside the ear – something which they absolutely love. The director of the zoo and his assistant were stunned to see the stallion with his head across my lap, obviously enjoying having his ears rubbed. I think they were probably confusing the Poitou with the Onegar or Somali wild ass as both of these species can be extremely difficult and dangerous.

The Galapagos Islands

On many of my visits I am accompanied by a vet and on this particular trip to the Galapagos Islands Bill Jordan came with me to try and sort out the problem of too many feral donkeys on certain islands which were threatening to destroy the eggs of the giant tortoise found only in this area.

On the trip down to the Galapagos Islands we had to land in Peru due to an engine failure and during our enforced stay at the airport we were fed on 'meat' sandwiches. A group of scientists from California were on the plane with us and by the time we arrived at the hotel in Guayaquil, the jumping-off place for the Galapagos, we were all suffering from extreme diarrhoea and vomiting. Sharing an experience such as this certainly brings out the best in people and we became quite good friends with the scientists before we all left to make our way on different tours.

The only way to reach the islands was by sea. The one problem Bill Jordan had when he accompanied me was his susceptibility to seasickness. Assured by travel agents that at the time of year we were travelling the sea would be flat and calm, we arranged to charter a small boat as this was the cheapest method of getting round the islands. However, we were to learn that we could not depend on the agent's assurance. From the moment we boarded the boat we had a force-six wind blowing and, with the strong currents between the islands, the sea was extremely choppy and uncomfortable. By the second day Bill Jordan had endured enough and he decided that once he got off the boat at the main island there was no way he was getting back on board again.

It took him three days to recover sufficiently even to think of continuing our work and we were racking our brains for a way to get out to Isabela and the other islands that we had to visit, when we had a real breakthrough. Walking along the street I suddenly recognized the people walking towards me as two of the American scientists we had met in Guayaquil. We stopped and chatted and they said they were on the only large boat that plies between the islands, which they had chartered themselves to study the various wildlife and fauna in the area. I immediately thought this could well be a way off the island for Bill and within two hours we had packed up and were welcomed aboard the scientists' boat. Despite this being much larger – it held fifty passengers – there was still a certain amount of motion. The scientists had already been on the boat for five days and as they were all very keen to be the first to step onto each island they had been split into three groups, the albatross, the boobies and the cormorants, named after birds on the islands. Day one, the albatross group would leave in the first

DONKEYS GO ON GUARD

Donkeys that bray and kick, rather than nod at the head of an oil well, have emerged as the latest boom business of Texas. It is not that the oil barons of Dallas have been reduced to riding the beasts in place of their gas-guzzling limousines after the collapse of oil prices, but rather that the donkeys have proved to be effective guards against the coyotes and boars that hunt on ranches.

The donkey, or 'jackass' in local parlance, began its new role in a desperate experiment by farmer Mr Perry Bushong, who has 20,000 acres of rolling land in the 'hill country' of central Texas near Mountain Home. The year before he had lost some 250 of his 3,000 Angora goats and Rambouillet sheep – worth some £50 each – to the wild dogs and boars when he heard an old folk tale about the effectiveness of the donkey as guard.

So he bought 10 donkeys from Mr Eddie Tom, a local horse trader, much to the amusement of his fellow ranchers.

Since then Mr Bushong has lost no livestock. Mr Tom has sold more than 75 donkeys, and the price of a good young female has doubled to nearly £200.

The young females, known as 'Jennies', have proved the most effective because when deprived of donkey company they adopt the sheep or goats as their own offspring.

Male donkeys, however, are inclined to attack goats as well as coyotes.

From *Daily Telegraph*, June 28th, 1986

© *The Daily Telegraph plc*

---

rubber boat and land ashore, followed by the boobies and the cormorants. Day two, the boobies would go first, followed by the cormorants and the albatross group, and so on.

Bill was not happy, even on the larger boat, and the first morning he struggled up on deck as the albatross group were just about to leave, looking particularly green around the gills. At this stage we hadn't been allocated to a group but the team leader, looking at Bill's very green face and the way he was gripping the rails gazing fixedly at the sea, decided that we should definitely be albatrosses that day. On stepping ashore we were able to watch sea lions at the closest quarters I'd ever seen them. In fact one of the party had a rather watery experience as he mistook a sleeping sea lion for a rock! Apart from this mishap, however, it was absolutely wonderful. Being with a such a knowledgeable group, including Bill who is an expert on wildlife, I learnt a great deal.

The following day it was the boobies' turn to step ashore first, but, once again, Bill's emergence on the deck, this time literally heaving, was enough to make us boobies for the day! For the rest of the trip we were automatically allocated to the first boat to go ashore, not only to Bill's relief but also to the relief of all the others who tactfully sat as far away from Bill as possible during the short trip to each island!

Dressed ready for work in England.

Greek Ouzo

Visiting foreign countries for the first time is always difficult; one has to learn new customs and new ways, and sometimes one can make the most stupid mistakes due to ignorance. This happened on one of our early trips to Greece.

Having arrived after a rather tiring journey, we went to a local taverna to get some supper. We were totally unaware of the type of liquid refreshment available but I had heard about Greek ouzo, so we decided we would ask for some. To our surprise they brought a bottle which they placed on the table and which we assumed we should drink. We did manage half the bottle but had no idea of the strength of ouzo and had rather assumed it to be more like wine. Anyone who has tried this local drink will know that it's one of the most powerful alcoholic beverages available! I had spilt some drops during the meal and only began to appreciate the strength of the ouzo when the varnish started to fade from the table and white spots appeared! When we came to pay the bill, to our surprise the taverna owner quickly measured how much we had drunk from the bottle and this is what we were charged for. He looked extremely surprised at the amount we had consumed and was thankfully very helpful in assisting us from our chairs. Not used to drinking, apart from the odd glass of wine, the effects of the ouzo lasted almost two days and our first experiences in Greece were rather muzzy to say the least. It is true to say that neither of us has touched a drop of ouzo since this first introduction!

Stranded

Working in Africa often poses unusual problems, particularly when travelling the islands in the Indian Ocean to worm the donkeys. When we visit the islands the team consists of a vet, Abdalla the manager of our Sanctuary in Lamu, June Evers, myself and a member of our staff. It is extremely hard and difficult work; the islands are scattered over an approximate eighty-mile range and we have to use a small motor boat provided by the hotel. We overnight at the furthest point. On this particular occasion we left the hotel at 5.30 a.m. and, having worked on three islands treating almost 700 donkeys, and covering over twelve miles on foot, we were exhausted. We arrived at our night's accommodation just after 7 p.m. The following morning we had to leave at 6 a.m. to catch the tide and, because the staff in the primitive hotel in which we were staying hadn't prepared any food for us, I spent a good time in their kitchen preparing a picnic for the day. We carried the picnic box out to the beach and it was loaded into the boat. We then left Kiwayu and went through the 'narrows', which become high and dry when the tide has dropped with only just enough water to scrape through, and landed at our first destination to treat a group of donkeys. Abdalla thoroughly enjoyed giving me a piggyback through the shallow water. I noticed that he and the boat man were rather quiet and after we had finished treating the donkeys and climbed back in the boat Abdalla said, 'Mrs Svendsen, we have a problem.'

'What is the problem, Abdalla?' I asked, and he explained that they had just tried to refill the almost empty petrol tank with the second drum of fuel, only to find, to their horror, that it had been filled with water instead of fuel. We didn't have enough fuel to get back to Lamu. We worked out that the tide would have dropped too far for us to get back to Kiwayu to refuel and the nearest other source of fuel was about sixty miles away. As the discussion deepened it became obvious that there was no way we were going to be able to get back through the inner side of the islands, where the sea is relatively flat, calm and protected, and our only hope would be to go out to sea through the bar and try and get round the shorter but rougher route before the fuel ran out. However, it was impossible to do that at the moment because of the heavy tide running and so it was decided to make our way to a sand atoll where we could wait until the tide turned. We would then have the advantage of a returning tide to try and make it back to Lamu. To get out to the atoll we had to go through a narrow cut with a heavy sea running but, fortunately, still with the tide. We decided that this was the only way out and with our small boat, slightly

Having a piggyback.

DONKEY DIAPERS BACKLASH

Efforts to devise suitable nappies to be worn by the donkeys of Lamu island off the Kenyan coast continue to bend the minds of citizens there, who have begun responding enthusiastically, it seems. The idea of providing diapers for the donkeys first surfaced early this year at a public meeting on Lamu, a popular holiday resort, which had been called to discuss ways of keeping the town clean.

Lamu has a large donkey population. The predictable result is much donkey dung. Hence the nappies idea. The Lamu district officer has just received the first three designs for such unlikely garments, two from men in Mombasa and one from a woman in Nairobi, which provides an opening for the tail.

But the idea has run into a snag – from the donkeys themselves, who have kicked up a fuss, evidently suspecting some people are seeking to make asses of them.

The MP for Lamu East, Mr Mzamil Omar Mzamil, told a political meeting that the donkeys had complained to him they were being harassed by the district officer. The donkeys said he should provide them for elephants, too, he reported.

From *Irish Times*,
March 29th, 1985
(Agence France Presse)

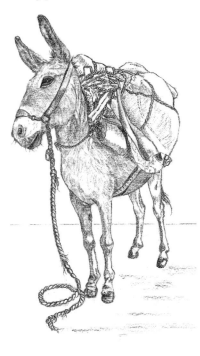

Ready for work abroad.

overloaded, set off through the channel to try to make the atoll where we could spend the day until the tide went down.

The boat almost turned over two or three times and I just jokingly said to June, 'Well at least we're all good swimmers,' when a shark surfaced within three feet of the boat, so close that its tail actually touched the boat as it went down again. All thoughts of swimming rapidly faded from our minds!

We were fortunate to make the atoll safely and there we spent six hours in the blazing sun waiting for the tide to turn so that we could attempt to get back to Lamu on the incoming tide. We were hot, burnt and very short of liquid by this time.

We eventually left at about 4 p.m. and nursed the engine with every ounce of fuel we could through the tanks. It was 6.15 p.m. before the engine puttered to a stop. We were in one of the most dangerous mosquito areas in the world, in a boat with no fuel, night fast approaching and little chance of any boat other than a sailing dhow coming within reach. For twenty minutes we drifted, and then a miracle happened. We heard the sound of a speedboat engine and coming across the sea towards us were three Dory type motor boats, on which, incongruously, were seated wealthy Italians on deck chairs enjoying an evening boat trip to see the sunset off Pate Island! They immediately came to our aid and we learnt that it was the first time this particular excursion had been organized by a group of Italians who had opened a small safari camp on the mainland. Our luck was certainly in, and they were able to give us just enough fuel to get back to Lamu.

In more ways than one it was close!

On a subsequent trip to Kenya we had perhaps an even closer shave. We were due to set off on the Monday, staying the night at our usual hotel in Kiwayu, when we heard the most disastrous news. On the Sunday evening a group of Somali bandits had crossed the border into Kenya and had attacked the hotel in which we were to stay, shooting the manager in the arm and raping women employees of the hotel. We were very pleased they decided to make their attack on the Sunday and not wait until the Monday when we were there!

Shower in Turkey

Travelling abroad always causes problems, as you can imagine, particularly in the Third World, where conditions for the animals are appalling and, for us humans, sometimes almost unbearable. Water is always a terrible problem, not only for drinking but also for washing. I remember many times as a child being delighted when, on our annual holiday on the Norfolk Broads, we had to conserve water and therefore washing became a non-priority event. However, working in countries amongst animals with the most terrible sores and diseases, and in frequent contact with humans suffering disease, washing is most important and the lack of any sort of water a real problem.

You can imagine our joy, therefore, when in one particular hostel we were told that although there was no water in the room, we could use the shower in the owner's private garden. June Evers was my companion on this trip and we both went out into the garden together and found the shower building they had erected had only three sides. You entered from the back, which was open, and stood under the shower with privacy secured from the house by the other three walls. Being very generous I suggested June took the first shower! I happily stood there holding June's dressing gown as she stripped off and was standing luxuriating in the shower, thinking it would be my turn in a few moments, when I became aware of a rather strange rumbling noise. Glancing behind me, to my horror, I found that the village bus had pulled up and what we had assumed was a high wall behind the garden was in fact the boundary to the main road. All the occupants of the bus had a full view of June's pleasantly rounded figure vigorously scrubbing away with her back to the appreciative audience! Without thinking, I called; 'June! My God, look behind you,' and she turned right around, giving a full frontal to the even more captive audience, who at this stage stood up in the bus and leaned out through the windows, shouting what we hoped were words of encouragement. I had never seen June try to get into a dressing gown so quickly in my life, and I don't think the fact that at this stage I'd starting laughing helped matters!

74

Home
from Home

Shelley, Mackenzie and Toby

Toby and Mackenzie are brothers and Shelley is a half-sister and the eldest at twelve years old. The three donkeys have never been split and came from a very good home in 1986 when a main road was to be built through their field in Northamptonshire.

Their owner was concerned that they would be split up but at the Sanctuary we are very aware of the strong bonds between groups of donkeys and the threesome went to our farm in Dorset. However, being such young, fit donkeys we felt they would benefit from being in a private home possibly with children and when a home was offered for three donkeys in Essex, and their stabling, fencing, etc, was approved by our Welfare Officer, Shelley, Mackenzie and Toby took up residence with Mr and Mrs Venus and family.

Peter Venus wrote this article on the donkeys for the Newport News *in 1988:*

When we arrived in Newport at the end of 1986, we promised our three children that we would put to good use the field that belonged to our house in Whiteditch Lane. The original idea of keeping donkeys has been claimed by each member of the family, but since I am the one writing about them I shall take the credit.

We contacted the Donkey Sanctuary in Sidmouth, Devon, and were told that under their rehabilitation scheme we could have donkeys on permanent loan if the facilities we had to offer were adequate. The Sanctuary rescues mistreated or unwanted donkeys and has over 3,000 of them. An inspector called and suggested that we should have a field shelter built and secure the fencing. This was duly done.

The Sanctuary rang a few weeks later to say that they had been given three donkeys, whose owner had to part with them as a result of a road being built through their field. They arrived a month later in a lorry and immediately seemed at home, our children following them every step of the way as they inspected the field.

Shelley quickly showed that she was the lead donkey, her brothers Mackenzie and Toby trailing in her wake. When rain appeared that afternoon the donkeys retreated in good time to their shelter, not emerging until the weather was clear. They remain the most reliable barometer I know for impending rain.

The donkeys proved fastidious in their eating habits, enjoying

The Venus children and their donkeys. Left to right: Maria Frances with Shelley, Benjamin with Mackenzie and Toby with . . . Toby!

carrots and apples but disapproving of cabbage and swedes. The children believed that this gave weight to their own likes and dislikes! First attempts at riding were not a success. The donkeys had been ridden at an earlier stage, or so we understood. Having purchased some saddles the first lesson we learnt was to sidle up to your donkey with great stealth. The donkeys, on seeing the family approach with armfuls of riding tack, immediately decided to explore the further regions of our field. One hour later the family regrouped to think again, the donkeys having thoroughly enjoyed our clumsy efforts to catch them. Carrots proved the solution, as often became the case. Munching contentedly, the donkeys were saddled with surprising ease and the children donned their riding hats in great excitement and climbed on board.

Then the hard part began. The donkeys wouldn't budge. They remained stationary whilst the children made the usual encouraging noises to start. You can't pull a donkey along. I've tried. Having referred to the donkey manual I went to the opposite end and pushed. Slowly Shelley changed into first gear and then the cavalcade got under way. Round the field we went very slowly until the field shelter again came into the donkeys' view and whoosh! off they went at a gallop. Three children hung on desperately as my wife and I gave chase. The children didn't reach the shelter at the same time as the donkeys. They had fallen off.

The donkeys still got supper that night. Riding got easier. They preferred head collars and lead reins to bridles and bits. Generally they are fairly quiet animals, although during their first night in Newport they gave us a noisy chorus at around three in the morning for several minutes. Mercifully that has not been repeated but occasionally during the day they will utter that extraordinary sound peculiar to donkeys.

Their differing temperaments and character have since become known. Shelley at ten years is older than her brothers and is the most placid and the easiest to saddle up. She is a skewbald (brown and white), whilst her brothers are brown. Mackenzie is the liveliest and the most inquisitive, and will follow you around the field, his presence suddenly being announced by a prod in the back with his muzzle. And Toby, the smallest donkey, although happy to physically push his brother and sister around, often gets more attention because of his large appealing eyes half hidden by a thick furry fringe.

DDD (donkey dung duty) is not popular with the children but is necessary to keep that part of the field clean which we have fenced off for the donkeys' regular use. A duty roster is posted in the kitchen and must be adhered to on pain of no pocket money. Whilst our donkeys are the cleanest of animals we regularly treat them with delousing powder and deworming paste and annual 'flu and tetanus jabs. The farrier calls every couple of months to clip their toe nails, since they are unshod.

The donkeys occasionally venture beyond their field. A trip to the pub along the bridle way means renewed acquaintance with the publican's goat. Visits this summer to the school fête and the street market to give children's rides seemed to be enjoyed by children and donkeys alike. Perhaps our next objective is to see if the donkeys could pull a small trap together. My wife, however is less keen to take the children to the primary school each day under donkey power, so maybe the trap would convey me to Audley End station instead!

Peter Venus

Twinkle and Molly

Twinkle and Molly were taken into the Sanctuary in 1986. A call from Wales alerted us to their plight; the complaint read 'I found three donkeys in a field who all appeared to have great difficulty in walking properly. Close examination showed that their hooves were extremely long and curled, and had not been attended to for a considerable time.' Our local Welfare Officer immediately visited. The donkeys had very long hooves and had no shelter. The three donkeys were signed over to the Donkey Sanctuary. Sadly, the gelding died after being with us for only a few weeks, despite intensive veterinary care. However, Twinkle and Molly, who are probably mother and daughter, recovered well.

Once fully fit, Twinkle and Molly went to live with Mr and Mrs Barwick who give them the love and attention they so deserve.

Extract from letter from Mr and Mrs Barwick dated March 17th, 1987:

I thought I'd drop you a line to let you know how Molly and Twinkle are getting along. They are both in good health and, as you can see by their picture, have splendid winter coats.

They seemed to settle in quite quickly although it was a week

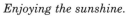
Enjoying the sunshine.

before they would set foot in their stable. I suppose not being used to any sort of shelter, it was all very strange to them. Once the cold weather set in, however, they were quite willing to be 'tucked up' for the night.

They are lovely creatures and have given us so much pleasure. We also have two dogs and two ducks and they all get along very well. In fact as soon as I let the donkeys out of their stable in the morning, the ducks go straight in and make themselves comfortable in the straw.

We are surrounded by farmland and tracks and so we

WHAT A DIFFERENCE A BRAY MAKES!

Whoever first decided that friend donkey merely says 'hee haw' was badly mistaken. We donkey lovers know that, as does any unsuspecting horse or pony exposed to donkey song for the very first time. Donkey song is unique. People love it, or they hate it. Other equines are awed by it. And much has been written and said about it down through the ages.

Donkeys actually communicate in a series of snuffles and wheezes and raspy inhalations most of the time. Occasionally they're inspired to let go with a true, full-throated bray – like at feeding time, for example. Or when a favourite pasture mate is taken away. Jacks often bray simply because they feel like it. Jacks are terribly vocal. They sing for the sheer joy of hearing their own voices. And what voices! What Jacks lack in vocal finesse, they make up in sheer volume. Jennets and geldings are far less likely to hoot and holler and carry on, reserving vocal exertion for special occasions.

And donkeys' brays do differ. Our three Bluestone Brayers' voices are not alike. Our boy Mordecai bellows like a pirate.

He builds up steam in a series of wheezy squeak-squeak-squeaks, then exhales a mighty yawwwwwwww that can be heard, plain as day, a good three miles across farm, field and forest. His big little buddy, Edward, is the tall, silent type. But when he sings, it sounds like the forlorn blast of an ocean liner in deep fog. Maudeen, elderly donkey matron that she is, seems to have never truly mastered the art of the successful bray. Her yawwwwww comes first, which leaves her totally breathless and hyperventilating in gasps and groans and wheezes. A neighbour, one who doesn't particularly relish hearing this asine chorus at daybreak, claims that the old hairy one sounds like a creaky iron gate when she brays – and she does.

There have evolved many folk sayings and proverbs regarding the donkey's bray. In Poland they say, 'If a donkey's bray is the first thing you hear in the morning, make a wish and it will come true.' Another states, 'The unexpected braying of a donkey is a sign of an unwanted visitor.' Two donkey proverbs include, 'Every ass loves to hear himself bray,' and 'If a donkey brays at you, don't bray back.' The raspy song of

the donkey has, in other places and times, determined gardening and weather conditions. In Eastern Europe, peasants used to say, 'It's time to shock the hay when Mr Donkey's heard to bray.' In Iran, people claimed that, 'When a donkey brays, the onions are sprouting.' Right here in America in colonial times, it was believed, 'When the donkey blows his horn, the weather is due to change.'

Donkey song has been discussed in some very ancient documents. Archaeologists, for example, unearthed a 4,000-year-old Sumerian clay tablet. On it, inscribed in cuniform lettering, were the words, 'My donkey was not destined to run quickly. He was destined to bray.'

Even the Bible has references to donkey song. Regarding the wild donkey, Job asked, 'Doth the wild ass bray when he hath grass?' Balaam, the prophet, had a talking saddle donkey, although she must have communicated in human words because Balaam understood her. She and the serpent in the Garden of Eden were the only talking animals in the Bible.

In Moslem legend, it is said that when Noah was rounding up animals to put on his ark, the donkeys tried to sneak the occasionally take the donkeys for a walk with the dogs with no worries about traffic.

Twinkle is the quiet one but Molly is quite mischievous sometimes, and has a real sense of humour.

Since their arrival, we have suddenly become the most popular aunt and uncle in the family! We have four nieces and nephews who think the donkeys are terrific. They were most interested to hear all about the Sanctuary and in particular the Slade Centre and asked us to send a donation in their names instead of buying them a Christmas present.

Devil aboard. Noah was angry, but he allowed the two donkeys to board anyway. As punishment, though, donkeys have had to bray any time they see old Satan lurking about.

Many folks are not enamoured of the donkey's bray. In India, for example, owners often slit their donkeys' nostrils to lessen the noise.

Shakespeare obviously didn't like to hear donkeys bray. In *Richard II* he compared trumpet blasts to donkey song when he wrote about 'the harsh-sounding trumpet's dreadful bray'.

In ancient Egypt, the donkey's bray was disliked. Still in existence is an ancient wall frieze depicting a slave guarding a herd of donkeys. One donkey has his head thrown up and back, nostrils distended, eyes closed, his mouth wide open in a throaty bray. The artist even painted symbols to represent the sounds of his song. The slave, a thoroughly disgusted look on his face, is waving his arms to silence the noisy beast.

But sometimes the donkey's bray historically came in handy. Herodotus writes that in a battle between the Persian cavalry and the Scythians, the loud braying of the Persians' donkeys and mules so frightened the Scythians' horses that, in the ensuing confusion, the Persians won the day.

Some of us, however, dearly love to hear the donkey sing!

One ancient Chinese nobleman, Wang Chuang Suan, so loved the donkey's bray that at his state funeral his dear friend, Emperor Wen, suggested that all present should imitate the donkey's bray as a parting eulogy!

Others have fully appreciated the song of our long-eared friends. In 1924, a poet known only as L.L.K. wrote, 'A donkey stands, he considers, he attains Nirvana, meets the riddle, solves it, comes back to Earth, and gives us the laugh.'

Sensing something meaningful in the donkey's bray, Henry Knibbs wrote in his poem, 'Burro': 'Your melody means something deep, unseen; Desert Contralto you are called; perchance an ear attuned to mysteries might glean more from your song than simple assonance.'

Desert Contralto is, indeed, one of the donkey's nicknames. Prospectors in America's Old West called him that, and also Rocky Mountain Canary. In Hawaii the donkey earned a similar nickname – Kona Nightingale.

In the June 2, 1871, issue of the *Denver Tribune*, there appeared an interesting and amusing tale of a backwoods preacher and a donkey's bray. It seems a fire-and-brimstone parson was winding up a rip-roaring sermon to his little country congregation. In conclusion, he threw up his hands, gazed beseechingly skyward and quoted from the Bible, 'Hark, I hear an angel sing!' Just then a donkey tethered outside the rural church let loose with a window-rattling blast. The good Reverend had a very hard time restoring order after that.

To the true lover of Mr Longears, there is real beauty in that raspy, throaty, resonant song. We can only agree with Wang Chuang Suan. To us, too, what a difference a bray makes!

Sue Ann Weaver, from The Brayer Magazine, *USA.*

Reprinted from the May, 1986 issue of *Midwest Equine Market and Horseman's Guide*; some quotations from Frank Brookshier's excellent book, *The Burro*, University of Oklahoma Press, 1974.

Hansel and Gretel Chester

Hansel and Gretel Chester come from Wales and were taken into the Sanctuary in 1984. Their owners were quite desperate; they had half an acre of land for the donkeys and during the drought were completely out of grass. They tried to purchase more land, without success, and matters got so bad during the drought that hay became unobtainable. They were frightened to sell the donkeys in case they ended up being sold for slaughter, and so the Donkey Sanctuary was contacted.

In 1985 they were out on rehabilitation to a home in Suffolk where they remained happily until 1988 when the family were to move home to a house with inadequate land for Hansel and Gretel.

'MAD COW' DISEASE KEEPS LIVESTOCK VALUE STATIC

My investment in livestock is creeping slowly up in numbers although, thanks to 'mad cow' disease, at best it is static in value. We have 131 cattle to enter in the June census and I am very glad to say we have a whole new livestock enterprise, for I have fallen heir to not just one but two donkeys.

Gina and her yearling son Dominic have come from a distant cousin who has given up his croft and did not want his cuddies to go out of the family. That suits me fine for, being in fierce competition with the other side for the affection of our grandchildren, there is no doubt having two cuddies gives us a distinct edge.

Now Dominic, being of an age when boy donkeys will start to be boy donkeys, and Gina not being with foal, the first job was to get her to an unrelated stallion. It so happens that our butcher has such a stallion . . . one with a particularly long and impressive record in the show rings . . . and he proved easy to deal with after a forty ouncer of malt whisky.

So on Sunday I was on the road waving goodbye to Dominic (who seemed to sense that he was being done out of something) and setting off to walk Gina the two miles to her holiday field where Gurgedyke Jockie the Fourth had some free time on his hooves and was waiting.

It may not have been the most important job I did last week, but it was certainly among the most pleasant and, as we clipped and clopped along the little road among the glorious broom, I was able to reflect on the irony of my mission.

Our cattle are currently in the middle of a state-of-the-art breeding programme in which we are taking ova from the eggs of heifers at the slaughterhouse, fertilising them in glass with Simmental sperm and implanting the resulting embryos into our Jersey cows.

Yet, here I was taking animal breeding back to the days when there was always a horse on the road to a coupling, though with the horse it was usually the stallion who did the visiting. I remembered the day 10 years ago when I took a bull over part of the same route to a neighbour's cow.

Daisy was a Shorthorn cross Ayrshire which provided milk for the house as well as for her own calf and three others. She was six months clear of her calf and still not pregnant, despite regular visits from the bull with the bowler hat. As Sandy said, 'This AI is a'right when it works, but it is a damn expense when it disnae.'

Sandy had asked me to bring one of my 'fancy bulls,' so I chose Glen Prosen who had been champion at the great Turriff Show, surely that would be fancy enough.

82

After visits by our Welfare Officer and veterinary checks Hansel and Gretel moved to live with Nicola and Andrew Combes.

In 1989 Nicola and Andrew wrote saying that as they so enjoyed having Hansel and Gretel could they care for two more! Zebedee and Sam joined the family and they are all getting on fine and enjoying life immensely.

End of Year Report from Gretel Chester: December 20th, 1988

Hansel and I moved here about nine months ago now, having spent four happy years with the Fishers at Eye in Suffolk. Training our new Caretakers has not been without its problems but I must say they are catching on pretty quickly now. Their lack of experience with equines in general was underlined several times in the early months when several quite unnecessary visits by the Veterinary

We were pleased to be striking a blow for traditional breeding methods and I felt it right that Glen Prosen should do his courting in his best clothes. I shampooed him, gave him a blow-dry, and combed his hair up with a little three-in-one oil so that he gleamed in the sun. We were a magnificent sight as we swung along the road ... me and my 14 cwt doggie on the halter.

As we passed the crofts on the way anxious neighbours peeped out, for news of our trip had gone before – and children had been warned to stay in lest they be gored by the wild bull.

Round the last corner we went and into the neat little close where Sandy and his sister Polly were waiting. There was Daisy rinking enthusiastically with a little Friesian heifer she had for company. We put Daisy and Glen Prosen in a loose-box and retired to the house for a business dram.

Soon we were sneaking back to see how the contract was progressing – but I'm afraid it wasn't. Glen Prosen

had, of course, no idea what he was there for, except that he could see that it was an occasion of some importance. And even though she had had 10 calves, Daisy had never been through that door either, as all had been by artificial insemination. There they stood, back to back, and looking distinctly bemused.

Polly was sure that nature would find a way and we retired to try another dram and discuss the decline in the moral standards of the youth of the day. Still there was no success and, while nature might indeed have found a way in time, we were impatient and decided to let them outside to rejoin Patricia in the field. Perhaps a *menage a trois* would be better.

Indeed it was. Being back with her playmate seemed to settle Daisy and the extra dimension fairly tickled the bull. Soon we had another business dram to celebrate and then we had another because we had acquired the taste for it.

When the bottle dried up I

caught my bull, waved goodbye, and set off for home in the glorious sunshine. The young bull gave never a backward glance, but his step seemed to have a firmer assurance as he strode rhythmically along.

As the sun beat down on us I put my arm across the great wide back and, resting my head on his soft warm flank, I shut my eyes and floated along. I could have slept on my feet there on the road.

In her own time Daisy had a fine heifer calf which, in her day, topped her section at the store sale at Maud. Glen Prosen went to Perth where he made me 1900 gns to add to the drams I earned when I introduced him to Daisy.

I hope the mating of Gina the donkey will be as successful. Certainly the welcome she received at her holiday field promised a successful outcome.

Charlie Allan
From *Glasgow Herald*,
June 18th, 1990

BRING BACK THE MULE!

Muffin the mule rides again . . . or at least that's what Mrs Lorraine Travis, of Hope Mount Farm, Alstonefield, is hoping.

Most people think of mules as stubborn, stupid creatures, the breed's only claim to recognition being brought about by Muffin, the puppet mule who danced across television screens during Children's Hour years ago.

But, claims Mrs Travis, the poor mule is much maligned – they are actually incredibly intelligent fellows, she says – and she and other enthusiasts in the British Mule Society have launched a campaign to Bring Back The Mule.

In America they are still very popular and can be bred to any size from Shetland to Shire for riding, driving and packwork says Mrs Travis, who founded the British Mule Society in 1978 and is its secretary.

She explains that their success in America is all down to big donkeys. A mule has a donkey for a father and a pony for a mother and in America they breed rather large donkeys. Now Mrs Travis and others in the society want to import bigger donkeys to raise the heights and hopes of British mules as working animals.

In ancient times mules were the chosen mount of royalty and aristocracy, and were rather revered creatures, and in the Middle Ages clergymen like Cardinal Wolsey used to trot about on them. They were still regarded as a status symbol up until the 18th century when, for some reason, they were used less and less, and their history since then has become obscure.

They were popular with the Army though, being regarded by soldiers as far more sturdy and less easily frightened than horses.

Says Mrs Travis, 'Mules in this country tend to be regarded as accidents. The Mule Society hope to try and encourage people to breed mules purely because they want them for a particular purpose, whether for riding, driving or work.

'Mules can do more work than horses on less and poorer quality food. They have a longer working life too and are less prone to illness and less likely to go lame.'

She goes on: 'They are amazing things really, incredibly intelligent – far more so than horses.'

But what about all these stories about mules being stubborn and nasty kickers? 'It's just not true,' retorts Mrs Travis. 'Mules are only stubborn and ill-tempered when they have been badly brought up! None of my mules would ever kick me.'

Mrs Travis believes that mules definitely have a big future in fuel-conscious Britain;

Surgeon were scheduled. As Veterinary Surgeons go I suppose Robert Lees is really quite a nice man but personally I do not care for their type and my man, Hansel, is quite terrified when anyone in a white coat and wellingtons shows up beyond the stable gate. However, such visits seem to be behind us now and for the last several months our new Caretakers seem to have been worry free.

When it comes to space and exercise we are really quite well catered for. We have a choice of three paddocks in all and these total about seven acres. On the minus side we are not allowed into two of the paddocks while they grow hay during the summer and, as far as I can see, during the winter while it is really quite wet we are kept out of the paddocks altogether and are confined to the stable yard. I think this has something to do with the fact that Hansel does love to roll in the mud incessantly when it is wet. The Combes have on occasions seemed quite upset at his appearance when he has rolled just a few minutes after a thorough brushing (if

numbers of mules are being purpose-bred and used for all manner of work. There is a place for them on smallholdings and for delivery work, but their main use will undoubtedly be for leisure purposes. They can be used for everything we currently use horses for and in many cases will do these things better. Farmers will opt for them instead of some machinery. Certainly the interest in mules has been renewed and is steadily growing.

From
Derby Evening Telegraph,
August 25th, 1980

only he was as smart as me he would wait until a more opportune moment).

Another criticism occurred during the summer when the grass was getting long and the Combes deemed that we had too much to eat. They had the local farmer put some cows into OUR paddock. The cows disappeared at the end of the summer but we are now saddled with three constant companions in the form of some rather woolly sheep. They are however quite good sports and Hansel will do his sheepdog act for half an hour at a time, chasing them around and around the paddock.

The best fun we had all year was on the two occasions that we escaped – although sad to say we only got as far as the garden as that is all fenced. On each occasion Mr Combes caught me first knowing that wherever I go Hansel will follow. However, on one occasion I did 'eyore' rather to Hansel and he took the hint and went running off around and around the house. I think Mr Combes was really quite frightened when he found that Hansel was looking in the swimming pool, obviously thinking of taking a quick dip. As he dragged Hansel back to the stables he muttered something about 'getting the bloody fire engine to winch him out'.

In another little episode Hansel managed to sneak into the feed store while Mr Combes's back was turned and picked up a fifty-six pound bag of carrots and ran out with them. A quick shake of the head and the carrots spread all over the stable yard – Mr Combes was quite surprised at how quickly we could eat them before he managed to pick them up.

We cannot complain about our creature comforts. The stable I suppose is adequate and they have this year had it double lined and insulated – the silly Farrier told them that it was better than most of those he sees for Race Horses! He must be a low grade Farrier if you ask me. Not only do we have to share our paddock with the sheep, we are now asked to share our stables with two farm cats. They are apparently meant to be good rat catchers, although all I ever see them doing is snoozing in the sunshine.

Christmas 1989: report from Gretel Chester
1989 started peacefully – on Maundy Thursday Hansel and I celebrated our 'official birthday' (we arrived at Lamarsh on Maundy Thursday 1988). It was a beautiful summer and, apart from the appearance of this newfangled fence which went crack everytime we touched it, we had a happy time. Whoever thought up electric fences as a method of enforced weight watching for Donks is no friend of ours! Summer ended with our keepers going away for three weeks (I am glad to say they remembered their manners and sent us a postcard) and the in-laws moving in to look after us. Life returned to the way it was when we first arrived here – we called, they came running! Oh, we led them a merry dance, but they thought we were wonderful and a happy time was had by all.

Then, on October 14th our life changed, almost as if a bomb had

Nicola Combes with Hansel, Gretel, Zebedee and Sam.

hit us (just as well we are said to be 'bomb proof'). Sam and Zebedee moved in next door. Sam, I soon realized, was almost as intelligent as me, and bigger too! Zebe was just enormous. However he did not care about his waistline (6′ 1″) and I am doubtful that he ever will.

At first my man, Hansel, was quite deferential to the new neighbours but of late he has forgotten that he is the smallest Donk and has become the 'school bully'.

The Little Donkey

I've carried many men before,
But none like this.
I step with pride, I'm strong and sure,
No step I'll miss.
His hand is gentle on my rein
A touch so kind,
The burden light and without pain,
Such joy I find.
I pace above a road of palms,
On polished hoof.
The people cheer and wave their arms
From street and roof.
We journey to Jerusalem
With none to sorrow
The crowds rejoice and cry 'Amen',
Will they tomorrow?

Joan Couzens

1990 started with us all becoming superstars – the WHOLE of East Anglia realized just how beautiful I am when a large article with photographs was published in the *East Anglian Daily Times* (EADT). My keeper has since been known locally as 'the donkey lady' and has referred at least one poor unfortunate to the Sanctuary. You will be amused to hear that when the EADT photographer arrived he thought that we would all pose in a neat row for him – just for the asking! He now understands Donks a little better and knows that 'Sam might eat your camera' was no idle threat.

A new vet has arrived at Taylor and Lees – Uncle Robert Lees doesn't come any more if he can help it but sends Cedric instead. Cedric is quite nice, as vets go, and bothers to learn our names and *ask* if we could be good. Sam is disgustingly friendly with Cedric – really lets the side down. Zebe, yes he of the 73-inch girth, amazes everyone by how elusive he can be when faced with a vet (or any form of medication) in a confined space. He has accordingly been nicknamed 'Twinkletoes'.

THE TRUE TALE OF BILLY THE DONKEY

Billy the Coastguard Donkey used to pull the small, traditional cart from the coastguard cottages at Bridgewick to the village almost every day. The accompanying coastguard would report to the village post office, owned by Mrs Pond and which stood adjacent to Rathescar in North Street and send in a report, for this village was one of the first to be given a telegraph service.

He would purchase provisions for himself and others and then, as shown in the photograph, would call at the Cap and Feathers to stock up with Baddow Brewery beer.

He would have been supplied by the landlord, seen at the door of the pub, who was a retired sea captain and was called Captain Cook. The donkey, I was told, was always well treated and the village boys and girls would make a fuss of it.

The coastguard cottages were built to combat the extensive activities of smugglers and the men would carry out routine patrols along the seawall.

The houses were in a remote area of the marshland and in the fifties they were demolished.

Like legends which grow, it is said that Billy the donkey's ghost still plods slowly along the cart track leading from the site of the houses to Round Barn Farm where the coal was wont to be left by the supplier to be taken when required by the coastguards.

Information and photograph supplied by Mr Jim Bye, which appeared in the *Maldon and Burnham Standard*, May 8th, 1990

Billy the donkey with cart outside the Cap and Feathers. (Photo from the historical collection of Mr H.J. Bye, c. 1905)

Storm and Skippy

Storm, a 6-year-old gelding, and Skippy, a 7-year-old mare, arrived at our Voluntary Welfare Officer's home from Northern Ireland in 1989. Although both donkeys' feet needed a trim they had been well cared for and had beautiful temperaments. The owner was moving house and could not take the donkeys with her. She had contacted the USPCA who had in turn contacted the Donkey Sanctuary.

The previous owner to the above contacted the Sanctuary and told us the past history of both donkeys she had raised from foals of nine and six months. It had been a heartbreaking decision for the family to part with the donkeys but a 'hooligan' element had caused problems and the lock on the donkeys' gate had been cut twice; living near two busy roads they were greatly concerned for the donkeys' safety. After several requests by people to purchase the donkeys the owner had eventually given them to a good home.

Storm and Skippy stayed for two months with our Welfare Officer as it was felt that to save a long journey to the Sanctuary a home in the north would suit them. Mr and Mrs Brooker offered a home to two donkeys just at the right time and Storm and Skippy are continuing to enjoy life in Sutherland.

Heilan Hee-Haw News 1 from the most northern rehabs
Irish donkeys in Scotland! Odd, you might say – but although they may hee-haw in a distinctly Irish accent, since their arrival at Tullich on October 9th, 1989, they've been very much at home grazing on yon bonnie banks and 'brays'.

Tullich means 'high place' and we are 750ft. above sea level with extensive views down the Kyle of Sutherland to the distant mountains of Canisp and Suilven. In fact, we are so high that our quarter of a mile of 'puncturesque' boulder-strewn approach track carved out of the hillside strikes fear into the heart of Krys Richardson, the Highland and Grampian regional inspector, everytime she pays us a visit. Not being acclimatized to the rarefied air of high altitude she usually relapses into a fit of the giggles as she drives up the track, while the acute angle of the Ford Sierra causes all her donkey paraphernalia to jump from the parcel shelf and land on her feet. How about letting her have a four-wheel drive vehicle – or a donkey instead?

Storm and Skippy are very happy in their new home and so far

Storm and Skippy – the Heilan Hee-Haws.

The routine pedicure.

there have been no attempts at donkey escapology. There's only one trouble – insurance. We can't get covered for 'Storm' damage.

Heilan Hee-Haw News 2 marking the first anniversary on October 9th, 1990, of the arrival at Tullich of the most northern rehabs

Storm and Skippy are both dangerously well and when the vet was here the other day, giving them their booster flu jabs, he remarked how very fit both donkeys looked. Since they were first led up our track to their new home a year ago they have ingratiated themselves into our lives and have become very much part of the family.

Our bathroom window is a waste-of-time window as it looks out over the large paddock, and while we perform our daily ablutions we are entertained by a varied repertoire of donkey antics ranging from an ingeniously choreographed version of the eightsome reel to just plain inquisitive staring up at the bathroom window, as if to say, 'What are you doing up there, and when are you coming out to give us our ginger biscuits?'

After carefully surveying our high security fences they have come to the conclusion a breakout would be impossible, so they've gone for the only other option – a tunnel! Digging started back in July and when the hole reached a depth of over a foot by September we decided the time had come to fill it in before the donkeys or ourselves slipped into it and broke a leg. We did a very neat job with one or two thick sods sprouting with nice fresh grass and the donkeys stood a few yards away looking on intently and admiring our handiwork. By the looks on their faces it was either food for thought or thoughts of food.

Within minutes of our leaving the field our repairs were turfed out and each animal had a neatly cut sward dangling from its mouth. Any subsequent infill work on the donkey tunnel will have to be done when they are in another field. Our only other problem is waste disposal and this can be summed up in one short verse.

> The trouble with keeping a donkey is trying to get rid of the dung,
> There's an elephant yield to a one-acre field.
> And weekly it's spread or it's flung.
> Now Sutherland's got a new mountain, a Munro with towering summit,
> The height of its peak rises ten feet a week,
> And it's only the donkeys who've done it!

THE DONKEY MAN OF LLANDUDNO

Donkeys have always been the mainspring of Llew Hughes's life and, even though he has officially given up his licence to his daughter Olwen, he still goes with her every night half-an-hour before sunset to the public field near the supermarket where they graze, to make sure that the donkeys are brought safely to their stable behind the house.

On fine summer days nothing can keep him away from Llandudno beach, where he is a well known local landmark.

As he has done for many years, he sits in his favourite chair by the slipway, watching the donkeys giving their rides to this year's crop of excited youngsters, just as their predecessors had done on the self-same stretch of sandy beach for over a century. The children he gave rides to 50 years or more ago are now grandparents themselves, and frequently they bring their families with them to meet 'the donkey man', and are very concerned if he is not in his usual seat.

Llew Hughes has been Llandudno's 'donkey man' for 70 years, so well known that letters addressed simply to 'the donkey man' have reached him safely from all over the world. The Hughes family are one of Llandudno's oldest families and a real donkey family, and Llew followed in his grandmother's and father's footsteps.

As well as Llew working the beach, his wife Ada, also 86, was alongside him for many years, and for a long time his three daughters Olwen, Gwen

and Margaret, also worked with the donkeys. Now Olwen is herself keeping up the family tradition and has taken over her father's licence and in turn is now known as 'the donkey lady'.

In the 1880s, Llew's grandmother Ann Hughes was one of the first donkey ladies of Llandudno. She kept a string of about six to eight mounts who worked a stretch of beach from the slipway to the White House Hotel. 'In those days it cost just two old pence a ride. Today about a century later, it has gone up 36 times to 30 new pence,' said Llew, a small, slight man with piercing blue eyes, who only gave up driving and riding a bicycle a year ago when his arthritis worsened.

Llew's father, Thomas, and his aunt Betsy, another famous local character, continued with their own strings for many years, and then Llew joined them with the rides. In those first early days he didn't have donkeys, but a string of about six to eight ponies on the West Shore. As soon as children broke up for their summer holidays, Llandudno became a busy resort and Llew not only gave pony rides to youngsters, but also taught them how to ride properly along the beach. He would be seated on the leading pony with a string of youngsters trotting sedately behind.

'Ponies are rather unpredictable, so I thought donkeys would be easier to manage,' he said. In 1940/1 he went over to Ireland and bought 13 sturdy young donkeys which he operated from the slipway.

'The price had then gone up

to six old pence for a ride,' Llew recalled. 'During the last war Llandudno was still a very busy place. Most of the big seafront hotels had been taken over by civil servants, but during the peak of the season there were always plenty of children wanting rides.'

Llew explained that there has been a great change in the pattern of holidays in Llandudno in recent years. Now, unfortunately, fewer young people are spending their annual summer holidays in the town, preferring to go further afield. 'Times have changed,' he said.

'We don't get the Sunday school trips or the people coming for Wakes Weeks, or as many day trippers. Now more elderly folk are coming here out of season, but when the children break up from school, providing the sun is shining and the tides are right, the donkeys are still kept busy. Donkey rides depend on the weather and the tides. If the tide is in we can't work, so if the tide is high most of the day, the donkey's don't leave their field,' he explained.

At one time he used to breed his own string, using a splendid white stallion donkey, Pinky, but unfortunately as more of the public land on which they graze was needed for development, breeding had to stop. Llew speaks of his donkeys with great warmth and affection and has always treated them with the utmost kindness. 'You can't make a donkey do something it doesn't want to do, but they do love their work,' he said, describing an incident of a few years back, when one

winter's afternoon there was a knock at his front door in Jubilee Street. 'Have you lost a donkey, because there is one on the beach,' said the caller.

When Llew went to investigate he found it was indeed one of his donkeys, who had decided she wasn't going to stay in the field but was going to work. So all by herself she had made her way to the deserted beach and was standing in her usual position by the slipway waiting for customers.

Llew and Olwen used to drive the donkeys from the field to the stable at the back of their house riding bikes and using sheepdogs, until the new one-way system of traffic put an end to the round-up, but now Olwen walks them back to the stable every night – which takes her at least half-an-hour, depending on whether they want to be caught.

The people of Llandudno and, of course, the visitors, feel that summer holidays wouldn't be complete without that most typical of seaside institutions, donkey rides! Llew is hoping that providing them will remain the Hughes' family business, and that in the future his grandchildren will run the rides, so that there will always be a 'donkey man' or 'donkey lady' of Llandudno.

From *Western Mail*, February 1987

Fred and Queenie

Fred's owner was moving from her home in Essex and the home she had found for him fell through at the very last moment. We were asked to help and took Fred into care back in 1983. He was gelded soon after arrival and in 1984 went out to a rehab home. There Fred met Queenie!

Unfortunately, Fred had to leave his rehab home in 1985 but Queenie accompanied him and was made over to the Donkey Sanctuary.

Later in that year both donkeys went out to the marvellous home of Mr and Mrs Freeman Dunn where they receive understanding, love, attention and humour.

Extract from a letter from Mr and Mrs Freeman Dunn, Will and Alex, dated January 30th, 1986:

I thought you might like to know how Fred and Queenie were getting along.

From the moment they arrived they seemed to settle straight in. They came quietly down from the truck, with my husband Paul leading Fred, and went (stepping up a small step) into a strange stable in strange surroundings in the dark with absolutely no qualms.

They were friendly with all of us from the start, spending a lot of time in those first few days examining the fencing and staring long and hard across the adjoining fields. I wasn't quite sure what was going through their minds!

My two children, William who's 3½, and Alex (Alexandra) who is now 20 months, took it all in their stride, as though having two donkeys delivered to the door at 6 o'clock at night was quite usual.

We didn't really get any 'problems' until about a week after they'd been here when we went down to Sheffield for the day to visit my family before Christmas.

I let F and Q out as usual at 8 a.m. and made sure they had sufficient water, hay and clean straw. The forecast was good so I knew they'd be happy grazing in the fields all day, and in any case the stable is always kept open so they can come and go as they please.

Our next door neighbour is the local gamekeeper, and he, or his wife, or their son, who works on a local farm, have often helped out by feeding the cats and ducks if we've been going out and knew we'd be late home. So I asked their son, Raymond, if he could get the donkeys in at tea time and make sure they had fresh hay and water.

When we got back from Sheffield at about 8 p.m. I just checked

Fred and Queenie.

that they were in OK and went and said a few words, but didn't find out until the next day what a job he'd had getting them in. He'd had to chase them all around the field and in the end called his father out to help him, and finally they rounded them up. And these are men with years of livestock experience behind them.

That following day Fred and Queenie would have nothing to do with me. They stood in the corner of one of the fields sulking all day. I went over to them with a carrot but they didn't want to know. They took the carrots but didn't want petting, and for about five days after that they gave me a hard time at 'bedtime', having to be chased around until I finally got them in. Fred was rarely any trouble, it was Queenie who seemed reluctant, and of course once Fred realized she wasn't going to come in, he'd turn tail and trot off as well!

Anyhow, it was all put down to experience. I'm glad to say that when we went away a few weekends ago, just for the day again, and I asked the same favour of Raymond, there was no trouble. They just went straight in for him, and the next morning things were as usual.

It has been interesting assessing their characters and

WANDERING HARRY RE-CAPTURED

Harry the donkey set Greenock on its ear when he decided to go out on the town. For he nonchalantly ambled up Union Street, neatly side-stepped two police patrols searching for him, and made his way to the juicy pastures of Caddlehill allotments.

Harry belongs to the Little Sisters of the Poor and is normally content to wander round his field behind their property in Union Street, Greenock.

But on Friday night his nocturnal wanderings were discovered when a passer-by asked one of the nuns if they owned a donkey.

When she replied 'yes' he told the startled sister that their pet was wandering along Union Street.

Sister Louise, who has looked after Harry since he arrived 10 years ago, immediately took up the chase.

'We went out with our van driver,' she said, 'and went up and down every street. Two police cars were out as well.'

By the time Harry left for his 'night out' darkness had fallen and fears were high that he might walk into the path of a car.

'You don't expect to see a big donkey walking towards you!' said Sister Louise.

Then word came in – Harry was holed up in the allotments and the police had him surrounded. They weren't taking any chances for he'd already made an ass of them during a previous daring escape. Four years ago a bid for freedom landed Harry behind bars after he broke a policeman's toe.

'He's well-known by the police,' admitted Sister Louise. 'He has a criminal record.

Since we've had him he has been out five or six times. Last time he went out he took off down Jamaica Street and when a policeman tried to stop him he broke his toe.'

On Friday night Harry finally gave himself up when he heard the familiar voice of the sister.

'When we got to the allotments,' said Sister Louise, 'he was surrounded by a lovely lady, three gentlemen and police officers. They walked him back down the road for me.'

'This time he's behind bars for good!' she said.

Harry, a sprightly, 19-year-old, was originally bought to keep the grass down but for many years has just been a pet.

'He is very popular with the children in the area,' said Sister Louise.

And an unrepentant Harry was enjoying a quiet horse-laugh in his paddock yesterday as he made plans for his next escape bid.

From *Greenock Telegraph*,
November, 1984

differences. And I'm afraid before they came I was always of the opinion that all donkeys look alike, but now whenever I see a picture of a donkey, or see one on TV, there isn't another that looks exactly like either Fred or Queenie. Queenie is a bit of a contradiction, because she tends to be the more timid of the two, but often the more friendly. She's always the one with her nose stuck out in the mornings waiting to be let out, and regardless of the weather, she has to push past me and stretch her legs, whereas Fred is always happy waiting in the warm, impatient for his morning hay. Queenie doesn't seem as keen to be groomed as Fred, and he stands patiently for ages while I fuss over him, and yet it's Queenie who comes up for the final word at 'bedtime', and pushes her muzzle into my face for a last bit of affection.

They love the Polos I give them as a special treat, and for

Christmas I bought them a packet of ginger biscuits, which went down very well. The children are forever raiding carrots out of the vegetable rack and wandering out with them.

Alex shows no fear of their size or noise (in fact the latter amuses her enormously and she tries to copy it), but I have to rather limit her contact with them, as Fred seems to have this compulsion to knock her over.

Soon after they came and I was mucking out with Will and Alex with me playing in the field, Fred came up very fast behind her, head down and ears back, and knocked her over and stood over her, which naturally upset her. I don't know why he did it, but Win Graham thought it was the kind of treatment he would give to a strange dog in the field, and that Alex is a bit too small to be around him.

Anyhow, obviously my first priority has to be to protect her, so I have to try to keep her right by me when I'm mucking out, which isn't easy because she likes to wander off and explore, and she also likes to go up and pat the donkeys. I'm just hoping they'll all get used to each other and Fred will learn she's no threat to him or his territory. Win Graham also thought there was a bit of jealousy about it as well, as she thought Fred acted quite differently when Alex was around. Anyhow, she's over the fright and the initial fear she had of them for a few days after that.

The day after Mrs Graham came we took F and Q out for a walk. They loved it. I was waiting for a decent day, when Paul was off work, so that we could manage it. I had Alex in the pushchair, Will walked (he had a 2-second ride on Fred but said he was going too fast!) and Paul took Fred and Queenie, or was it they who took him for the walk?

At first we took them down through the woods at the bottom of our fields, but when we came to a narrow wooden footbridge over a beck they point blank refused to cross, so we backtracked and took them down to the road at the end of our track and up the hill to see friends of ours at a nearby farm who had expressed an interest. She must have been keen, she got off her sick-bed (she was in the throes of pneumonia, which I hadn't realized) to come out to see them, and was thrilled. She's taken all the rehabilitation info off me, so who knows? She may also be getting in touch.

But most of all it was Fred and Queenie who enjoyed the walk. I thought they'd keep stopping to eat from the hedgerows, but they pricked up their ears and kept striding out, eager to get on. I hope we'll be able to take them again soon.

We passed two horses in a stable yard who seemed very interested, so we took them over to say hello. The smaller of the two horses came over – Fred promptly bit her on the nose! We made a hasty getaway!

Clem and Matt

Back in 1980 a supporter rang the Sanctuary to ask if we could help as she had just purchased two young donkeys at Exeter Market, one of which she felt was in a poor condition. Both donkeys were taken into our care and received the veterinary attention they needed. They were approximately three years old. Incidentally the lady, Jane Scott-Fox, became one of our Voluntary Welfare Officers and has been with us ever since.

A lady had recently visited and asked if we could name a donkey after her late husband who cared greatly for donkeys. The skewbald gelding was therefore named 'Clem' after her husband and the grey donkey was named 'Matt' at the request of a dear old lady of 83 as this was her childhood nickname.

In 1982 the donkeys went to Yorkshire to the home of Mr and Mrs Wright, where they joined a horse, a Dexter cow and dogs. Clem and Matt have been with them ever since and are definitely part of the family. After a hard beginning in life they now have total security.

Extract from a letter from Mrs Wright dated November 1st, 1982:

I understand from Mrs Graham that the donkeys had a long and not very pleasant journey from the Sanctuary to Yorkshire due to the high winds at the time. However, they settled down very quickly, joined our hunter mare in her paddock and were all eating together quite amicably within about one hour.

Within twenty-four hours we discovered that Clem, the skewbald, although the smaller of the two, was the boss, especially with his hind legs. In fact the mare has learnt to keep her distance from him.

About ten days ago, when the nights grew rather cold, with a touch of frost, we decided to bring the donkeys into a stable at night, and leave the paddock and field shelter to the mare. Within two days Matt found his voice and became the spokesman, letting us know each evening when he thinks they should be coming in for their carrot, pony nuts and bran mash mixture in their stable. So you will see that they have become part of the family and even appear to be putting on weight, although it may be just their winter coats.

Peanuts

In March 1986 Peanuts arrived at the Sanctuary from Essex. He was ten years old and his owner found him difficult to handle.

After some training we felt as Peanuts was a young donkey he would benefit from the individual attention he would receive in a home. We did not want to send him to a home with children as we felt he would not enjoy being fussed too much and it was considered Mrs Susan Webster's home would be ideal as she was conversant with the needs of equines. So five months after arrival at the Sanctuary Peanuts was delivered to Lancashire as a companion to Mrs Webster's horses.

Peanuts was not easy to cope with in the early days and tried out 'all the tricks' but Mrs Webster has persevered and he has settled down well and now has Ben as company.

Peanuts, Ben, Mr Webster and son and their friend the cockerel.

Extract from letter from Susan Webster:

Just thought it was about time I wrote to let you know how Peanuts is doing. It has been a long time since my last letter, but what an eventful time. Peanuts had settled fine with the two horses when a 'so-called' friend dropped a note through my door (Christmas 1986) to say there was a seven-year-old donkey at a local farm that was being sold for meat and could I take him? I knew the donkey (Ben) did once belong to a small children's zoo and was used to a lot of attention. I rang the Sanctuary and explained the situation, and asked if I bought Ben and had any problems with him could I pass him on to the Sanctuary? (to which the answer was 'Yes'). As it was December and Ben had been living outside he did have a slight mud rash though apart from that he was in good condition. We brought Ben home about two days before Christmas Eve; he is such a quiet donkey I was a bit worried in case Peanuts bossed him. After a good look at each other they were fine.

I think Ben must be the strong silent type as no matter how much Peanuts fusses Ben doesn't bat an eyelid.

After a couple of weeks, we decided to take them both for a walk, as we had been used to doing so with Peanuts. We have a public footpath directly opposite our house which has car access for a few houses dotted along the track. We had also found out that we were going to have a two-legged addition and at the time I was about five months' pregnant, so it was decided I would lead Peanuts and my husband would lead Ben. Carrie our dog went off in front, followed by myself and Peanuts and John with Ben. The next minute next door's horses decided to charge round their paddock. Ben decided it was a stampede and set off, Peanuts thought he was being charged at and went into a canter. I gave a discreet 'whoa', then a less discreet 'whoa', then a 'whoa' to alert the neighbourhood. My husband, not being able to pull Ben up, had flung himself round Ben's neck and dug his heels in on the gravel path. Feeling decidedly un-athletic and wondering how long I could maintain a canter, it flashed through my mind – devastation of farmer's crops and neat front gardens, all brought about by donkey hooves. Luckily John's tactics worked and Ben pulled up. Peanuts did likewise. I was, to say the least, relieved. Carrie had been so frightened she'd run quite a long way and it was a while before she got back to us. We turned round, and gingerly made our way home. It seemed a very long fifty yards.

In July 1987 our son was born. I couldn't wait to introduce him to the donkeys and horses. I don't think they appreciated the noisy bundle. Now he is twelve months and I take him down in his pram to meet them. The donkeys are very nosy and stand either side of the pram letting him pat them. The only problem is when they decide to get hold of the pram with their teeth, I don't think Silver Cross thought of making it donkey proof.

The donkeys have another friend that we acquired by accident, a cockerel. He thinks he's a bit special and insists on riding around on the donkeys' backs. Ben and Peanuts don't mind at all and if one of them stands still for too long he hops over to the other one, hence we call him 'the Jockey'.

Though Ben and Peanuts get on together I don't think they would miss each other as Ben often grazes with my horse and Peanuts seems to like humans better, though he won't be fussed over. Ben will stand and be groomed forever, while it's an effort to get Peanuts to be brushed.

▼ ▼ ▼ ▼ ▼ ▼ ▼ ▼ ▼ ▼ ▼ ▼ ▼ ▼ ▼ ▼ ▼ ▼ ▼ ▼

'I'll help you.'

Jack Melrose

Jack came into the Sanctuary in 1982 as a seven-year-old stallion when he was, of course, gelded. Jack had come from a good home and had been rescued by his owner but they realized that he needed the companionship of another animal.

By the end of 1983 it was felt that Jack would benefit from being out in a home with individual attention, provided that he had a companion, as he had fought other donkeys when put in a large group. Jack and Mrs Lightfoot's horse, Prince, a retired police horse, lived in complete harmony.

Sadly, Prince died in 1987. Mrs Lightfoot had by then purchased another pony but Jack was extremely difficult for some time until Jenny, a mare donkey from the Sanctuary, joined the family. The threesome are now extremely content and Jack gives the occasional ride to Mrs Lightfoot's handicapped nephew who squeals with delight on seeing Jack.

Jack, Mrs Lightfoot and Prince in 1985.

102

Extract from letter from Mrs Lightfoot dated October 4th, 1985:

We took delivery of Jack Melrose on September 14th, 1983. The donkey was at first very wary of my 16.2 hh gelding (a retired police horse called Prince). However after a few days, they settled down and are now very firm friends. They each become very worried if the other is out of sight. They have adjoining stables, and from the first little Jack Melrose took charge. He looks like a cuddly toy next to Prince, with his broken coloured coat, one would swear that he had been knitted!

I did not know that the hunt was in our area, otherwise I would have put them in the stables. They were out grazing in the field (or so I thought) when I received a phone call from the local police (who knew the horse and donkey – and me).

He said, 'Do you know where Jack and Prince are?'

'Yes, in the field,' I replied.

'They are not, they have joined the hunt, you'd better come and get them,' he laughed.

My son and I rushed around in the car with the head collars, to where the hunt was meeting. I wish I had had time to collect the camera too, because the sight was hilarious. There was the hunt with the immaculately turned out horses and at the back were Jack and Prince. Jack's coat was long, shaggy and dirty, and Prince (by now rather old and gaunt) in a tattered New Zealand rug, from forcing his way (after Jack) through a thick hawthorn hedge. I shall never forget the sight . . .

Extract from welfare officer's report:

Jack has really settled in very well indeed and to see him with the police horse is quite something – David and Goliath in fact! They are very attached to each other, and Mrs Lightfoot is delighted with Jack . . .

When we got there this time, the goose was bathing in a tin bath, the twelve sheep all came to the garden steps, making an awful din as they begged for grass nuts, both labradors nearly knocked us down, and when we went in the field Jack and Prince came bounding towards us – stepping out of the path of a 16.2-hand horse and a joyous donkey is quite an experience! A very happy animal home.

Extract from letter from Mrs Lightfoot, dated October 5th, 1990:

A Poor Man's Tale

Upon a cold and bitter night
I was to see a wondrous sight
So gather round friends, young and old
I have a tale which must be told.

My little donkey, small and grey
Had left his stall and gone astray
I searched for him so hard and long
But could not find where he had gone.

All at once, my friends did cry
'Come hasten here! See what we spy!'
With dread I hurried down the hill
For could it be that he was ill?

At last I came to a stable bare
And saw that gentle beast was there
Softly he blew upon the hay
Where in its warmth a baby lay.

That tiny babe gazed up with love
And angels sang from far above.
At his feet three wise men knelt
And with respect showed how they felt.

With my donkey an ox did keep
A watchful eye as the babe did sleep.
While by his side a maid did pray
Then asked that one and all should stay.

When at last the baby stirred
From his lips a sound was heard.
My donkey, resting by his side
Gazed gently at him as if with pride.
And then the child did touch his back
And lo! we saw a mark of black.

All who saw it turned to me
And said as one, 'You must agree
That ne'er again will your beast be lost
For now he bears the mark of the cross!'

From that day all donkeys bear
The cross I saw so plainly there.
A sign that his Master in heaven above
Has ne'er forgotten a donkey's love.

Sally-Anne Hardie

Fund-raising

I mentioned in the Foreword to this book that there are lots of ways in which people can raise funds, not only for our charity but for other charities as well, and the following pages are full of suggestions and information – from the regulations on collecting for charities to such simple things as how to run a successful stall, methods of costing when running coffee mornings and similar, and different ways in which people have raised funds for our charity in particular. Don't forget, fund raising should always be fun as well as having a more serious object in view; very often, in the course of setting up different ways of raising money, you'll be surprised at the number of new friends and acquaintances you make, and how you are able to change your life-style, possibly for the better!

Fun during a Royal visit.

How to Help the Donkeys

Donations: Many people prefer not to organize events and would rather give a straightforward donation which is, of course, most gratefully received indeed.

Covenants: If you pay Income Tax then a payment under Deed of Covenant is the most beneficial way of making a donation as we are able to claim an additional amount from the Inland Revenue at no extra cost to the donor or our charity. A Deed of Covenant means that the donor promises to make a specified donation to the charity every year, for a minimum of four years. Forms can be obtained by contacting the Sanctuary and advising which of our charities you would like to help in this way.

Give as you earn: For those in employment an arrangement can be made whereby your employer deducts from your pay packet a weekly/monthly sum to be paid to the charity of your choice. The deduction is made before calculating PAYE.

Gift aid scheme: This is a new scheme whereby individuals or companies may give a single, one-off donation of £600 or more per annum on which the charity can then reclaim tax from the Inland Revenue. Donors need to complete a tax certificate which can be obtained from the Sanctuary.

Collecting Boxes: Cardboard collecting boxes are available, for all of our charities, i.e. the Donkey Sanctuary, the International Donkey Protection Trust, the Slade Centre and the Elisabeth Svendsen Trust for Children and Donkeys and can be obtained on request.

Collections should only be made, however, from your own home or your own business. Many of our supporters keep a collecting box in the hall of their home for visitors, at their office, on the counter of their pub or shop, or at the reception desk of their hotel, on their market stall, etc. Street collections and door-to-door collections cannot be made.

When the collecting box is full you can either count the monies and send us an equivalent cheque or deliver the collecting box to us when you are next in Devon visiting the donkeys.

Purchase of goods: A sales list can be obtained from the Sanctuary of books and cards produced. The purchase of these helps the charities immensely.

Promotional material: If you would like to receive collecting boxes, posters, newsletters or leaflets for your event we are happy to provide these free of charge.

We are also prepared to provide our books and cards on a 'sale or return' basis.

If you are giving a talk to a local WI group, Rotary Club, etc, then we will willingly lend you a video of our work in this country or abroad.

Sponsorship:
Swims
Slims
Walks
Marathons and half-marathons
Horse/pony rides
Silences
Cycle rides
Parachute jumps
Shaving off beards/hair
Schoolchildren paying to wear their own clothes to school instead of uniform

These are just some of the ways our supporters have raised money and they are very successful means of raising funds.

Sponsorship can be obtained from friends and acquaintances and sponsorship forms can be handwritten or typed. Do make sure you do not undertake more than is physically possible and if children are involved do make sure that the activity is safe.

Your sponsorship form should be drawn up on these lines:

Sponsorship Form for Anne Scott to walk 20 miles on 4th March from Priory Park to Bishopstown in aid of the Donkey Sanctuary of Sidmouth, Devon.

Name	Address	Amount per mile	Total	Date paid
....	....	....	....	....
....	....	....	....	....
....	....	....	....	....
....	....	....	....	....

Sales: Fairs and fêtes are a good way of raising funds, but there are other ways of selling, i.e. children producing sweets and cakes to sell at break time at their tuck shops; jumble sales; garage sales; car boot sales; market stalls; coffee mornings/evenings; sale of home-made cakes; quiches, etc, at the office; sale of bedding plants and fruit from gardens; sale of horse and donkey manure; sale of crafts.

Raffles: Raffle books can be purchased at stationers and tickets sold at say 20p each or five for £1. It is fine to run a private small raffle amongst friends and there are no restrictions.

At a fete, dance or other small 'do' tickets have to be sold at the event and should not be sold beforehand to stay within the law. In addition there should be no cash prizes and the prizes must not exceed £50 in value in total. You cannot advertise the raffle in advance nor can you deduct expenses from the profits.

Larger raffles should not be considered where tickets are sold to the public and tickets printed as application has to be made to register with the local authority in accordance with the Lotteries and Amusements Act 1976.

Examples of payments donated to the donkeys: The donkeys have benefited from many diverse activities such as:

- Payments from friends for watering plants whilst on holiday, feeding cats or birds.

- Dog walking.

- Baby-sitting.

- Swear boxes.

- Opening of gardens for a day.

- Donkey rides (of course, only to children under 8 stones).

- Donations in lieu of flowers at funerals.

- Donations in lieu of Silver/Golden wedding presents, retirement presents, birthdays, Christmas presents.

- Donations given to supporters for talking at W.I., Rotary Club meetings, etc.

- Money saved in giving up sweets, cigarettes, etc, for Lent.

- Church collections

There have been other more unusual methods such as monies received for the display of a beautiful doll's house at a stately home; donations received for the display of a statue of Blackie, signatures embroidered on a tablecloth and payment made to write each name, etc.

Waste not want not: Every two years during August we hold a festival at the Slade Centre: an afternoon of stalls and games and, of course, lots of donkeys. All profits made on the day go to help the general running costs of the Slade Centre. We are, therefore, most grateful for bric-à-brac, jewellery, crafts, toys, books, etc, to sell on the day. These goods can be sent to us at any time or if postage costs would be prohibitive we can arrange for collection through our Welfare Officers.

The Donkey Sanctuary is most grateful for used stamps; which are sorted and sold to raise funds for the donkeys.

Green Shield stamps and Co-op stamps are also gratefully received.

Air Miles are used by the International Donkey Protection Trust for their visits to help donkeys abroad and substantial savings can be made on travel costs.

Sponsor a donkey: We are frequently asked by supporters if we run a sponsor a donkey scheme. Apart from in a small way through children helping to sponsor Frosty, Pancho and Ruff and individuals and organizations sponsoring donkeys at the Slade Centre, the answer is no. We have considered the matter in depth and feel that the administration costs involved in writing to inform sponsors of the welfare of their particular donkey or, for example, the movement of their donkey to one of our other farms, would outweigh any of the financial benefits from sponsorship. We are always very aware that our supporters are donating money to help the donkeys and we therefore keep our administration costs to the absolute minimum. Annually an independent survey is carried out by the Charities Aid Foundation and the Donkey Sanctuary's administration overheads accounted for only 4p in the £1 in 1989; thereby ensuring that monies go directly to where they are intended – to the care of the donkeys.

The approximate cost for the keep of a donkey for one year is £625. At the Slade Centre, where our specially selected group of donkeys give rides to the handicapped children, some of the donkeys are sponsored and this, therefore, helps not only the donkeys but the children too.

In memory: If you are able to consider remembering one of our charities in your Will this would really be a great help to us but we hasten to add that we hope it will be many years before we benefit. In recognition of this kindness we inscribe annually on our Memory Wall at the Sanctuary the names of all those who have helped our charities in this way.

The suggested wording for Wills is along the lines as follows: I give and bequeath unto the Trustees of *The Donkey Sanctuary/ The IDPT/The Slade Centre/EST, Sidmouth, Devon EX10 0NU the sum of £ .... for the general purposes of *The

CASH A COMFORT FOR TOPSY

An article in the Advertiser about Topsy the Donkey brought an overwhelming response to a fund raising venture.

Topsy, the former children's favourite at the old Holly House nursery in Aughton, now lives in a donkey sanctuary in Devon.

An old friend of Topsy's, Grace Hetherington, of Moss Delph Lane, who was matron at the home, organised a fund-raising fete to help keep him at the sanctuary.

'The response was quite overwhelming and we have £732 to send to the sanctuary.

We are very thrilled and grateful to everyone who contributed,' said Grace.

From *Ormskirk Advertiser*, September 1987

Donkey Sanctuary/The IDPT/The Slade Centre/EST and declare that the receipt of the Administrator or the Deputy Administrator or other proper officer for the time being of the *The Donkey Sanctuary, The IDPT, The Slade Centre, EST shall be a sufficient discharge to my Trustees.

Very often friends and relatives wish to have some sort of memorial to a loved one and at the Donkey Sanctuary we are always happy for a tree, shelter or bench to be donated in memory of the deceased and a plaque erected.

* Insert the charity you wish to benefit as monies can only be allocated to the charity you state.

Fêtes, Fairs, Festivals, Coffee Mornings

The following hints apply whether you are having a stall in your garden or filling a field or hall. It has to be fun for helpers and visitors. Everyone has to know what they are doing and be made to feel comfortable and that they are genuinely being a great help, however small or large their contribution. No matter how flustered you feel as organizer it must not show – a huge smile and the continual muttering of 'No problem' and 'That looks lovely' is a must! If you are happy, confident and enjoying the event – then it will rub off on your helpers. The greatest help is if someone offers to bring the whole stall stocked, run it and give you the takings. The next best is that you organize the stall, stock it and someone runs it for you – but they must feel confident of what they have to do, so explain fully the workings of the tombola, catch-a-duck, hit-a-teddy, etc. Make sure they have everything they need: pens, paper, tickets, prizes, basket or tombola tub and something to sit on. Some lovely people will bring all this but it's up to you to make sure they know who's doing what! Never bully helpers or make them come out of a sense of duty! They'll come but the feeling is not the same and they may find an excuse for next year!

Committees can: (a) Share the work happily or (b) Cause a lot of aggro when Mrs A takes over what Mrs B wants to do – so you have to be one hundred per cent diplomatic. If you can foresee trouble, don't form a committee, just ask friends to do different tasks – teas, raffles, stalls, entrance money, treasurer (unless you do that too). After the first event you will have an idea of who's good at what.

Raffle – it's no good having a quiet person on a raffle! You need a dynamic (noisy) person who doesn't mind accosting people! Raffles really shouldn't have too many prizes and they should be clean, tidy and well displayed.

However long your event lasts, and whatever it raises (as long as it is profit!), if everyone goes home happy, then it was a good 'do' and, who knows, it could be bigger next time – if you can face it – and if you've enjoyed it then you'll face it again.

Do make sure you thank absolutely everyone and tell them the amount raised.

With larger fêtes, fairs and festivals – one or two day events – it is essential to start planning months in advance. Do organize extra help to cover for rests and breaks. I don't agree with everyone stopping for a three-course lunch and wine but people do need a cup of tea and a bun or time to eat their picnic.

If you have celebrities or attractions, remember they all cost money and stop people spending their money whilst they are watching them – so not too many and not too expensive. You will also need people to 'shepherd' celebrities or attractions – they mustn't be left to find their own way around.

Before the day send everyone a plan showing their stall, car park, times to come in, programme of events, loos (most important), time of raffle draws and where the treasurer will be. The tone of your accompanying note is important to get them in the mood – it may even be an idea to ring up.

On the day you will have the hardest job, be there early, make sure everything is ready. Tables and chairs (if applicable) should be set out, covered with white sheets or crepe paper, and/or decorations and bunting put up well beforehand. Never over-price – people will spend much more if they think there are bargains. Of course, if Mrs C has given you items and priced them, then that price has to stand. Different areas have different price levels and the last thing you, the organizer, wants is to take home lots of

Leslie Crowther, Elisabeth Svendsen and winner of the Fancy Dress Competition at Slade Centre Festival.

unsold goods to store till the next time. Your house may never empty of bric-à-brac!

Have someone on duty for drinks or tea for the helpers – that person could check all is well and that everyone has enough of everything – a general jollier-along! – but choose your person carefully. You, as the organizer, should be generally checking everyone, everywhere all the time (it's great fun!).

Aprons with large pockets for money (money aprons) can be hired or made and are much better than money dishes that can be pinched or tipped up and you have to keep moving from your place to get change, etc.

If there is to be an official opening then keep the public out until then – if it's a celebrity appearance at a set time, then set your opening time and be prepared for selling from the first minute – you may lose pounds if a stall-holder is late opening or is off getting change or finding the loo!

Sign post everything clearly – naming stalls can add to the fun,

113

i.e. 'Freda's Freshly Made Fudge' – 'Harry's Home-Grown Apples'.

Programmes can raise funds but only if you can get them printed free or cheaply. Lucky programme numbers can encourage sales – but it is only worth the worry if the sale of programmes covers the prize plus printing and gives you a profit.

Peaks of Bournemouth sell/hire complete stalls and give good instructions but if you can fill a stall free and then sell everything that equals more profit for the funds.

Julie Courtney

A Profitable Coffee Morning

The best profit will, of course, be obtained if you can persuade friends to donate the coffee, milk, sugar and biscuits! However, if this is not possible, do not try and economize by purchasing cheap coffee; you only need to use more and the results are not good.

● If you are warming the milk for the coffee do not boil this as the milk volume reduces considerably when a skin forms.

● Warning – children like eating sugar lumps and these can disappear rapidly! Brown sugar is expensive so granulated sugar is the most economical.

● Likewise homemade biscuits are 'more-ish' to both children and adults, the ingredients can be expensive and they take a considerable time to make. A higher profit will be obtained from shop-bought biscuits.

● You can estimate that one cup of coffee costs 6p and allowing for purchase of the biscuits, payment of gas or electricity and possibly rent of the hall, the approximate cost is 10p. Therefore, if a charge is made of 25p or 30p per cup of coffee, including biscuits, a good profit will be made.

● If you have a produce stall do not overcharge for cakes, vegetables, preserves, etc. People like to get a bargain and are more likely to buy more if the prices are below shop price.

● You may like to make your coffee morning more of a 'flea market'. Coffee and biscuits can be sold by you and your helpers and produce stalls run. Sell as many tables as you can fit into your hall for £2.50 each to other groups or charities for them to sell whatever they wish and keeping the profit themselves. The income you receive from the sale of the tables will pay for the rent of the hall and the money received from coffees and produce will be profit.

Sheila Rabjohns

CARROTS

A donkey's favourite food — and can be enjoyed by humans too. Plant a row or two in your garden as a treat for the donkeys. They are not the easiest vegetables to grow, but here are some simple instructions to follow:

Growing carrots from seed
First the soil must be right: carrots will not thrive on freshly manured ground, since then you end up with forked roots and wiggly shapes. So grow them in soil that was manured last year; poor soil is equally bad, since you will just end up with tiny ones. Work the soil so that it is well broken up. Sow the seed from March onwards, dropping two seeds per inch, a quarter of an inch deep in the soil in rows one foot apart. Rake the soil over the seed and put a line of black cotton over the top so birds don't bathe in the fine soil; and then sit back (do NOT touch them) until the first week of July. Then thin the carrots so that they are three inches apart and a couple of weeks later to six inches apart. By 'thinning', we mean gently pulling out the clumps of carrot seedlings, leaving one to grow big. You can eat the spindly ones you have pulled out, they are rather delicious (or give them to a nearby donkey). If it is difficult to pull the thinnings out, use a kitchen fork. Harvest the rest of the carrots just before the first frosts in October and store them either in sand or dry soil. Feed throughout the year to four-footed friends.

Recommended varieties:
(early) Nantes Champion Scarlet Horn, Amsterdam Forcing (maincrop) Chantenay Red Cored, Autumn King.

Other varieties include Large rote stumpfe ohne Herz Sino — which has appeared in the Guiness Book of Records as the world's largest carrot, Bertop (good as early and main crop), Flamant (recommended for beginners), Jasper (good for salads), Minicor (baby carrots) or Suko (can be grown in window boxes).

Carrot cake
1 teaspoon cinnamon
1 teaspoon mace
½ teaspoon salt
4 oz (110 g) butter or margarine
½ pint honey
4 eggs
4 large carrots, grated
8 oz (220 g) flour
3 teaspoons baking powder
just under half a pint of hot water
4 oz (110 g) chopped nuts
Cream the butter and the spices, gradually adding the honey and beat well. Then add beaten eggs and grated carrots. Sift baking powder with flour and add to carrot mixture, alternately with hot water. Add nuts. Put in a greased 9″ × 13″ tin and bake 35 minutes at 350°F, gas 4. Ice with cream cheese icing:
6 oz (170 g) cream cheese, softened
½ teaspoon vanilla essence
12 oz (340 g) icing sugar
1 – 2 tablespoons milk
Beat the cheese till smooth, then add vanilla and gradually beat in icing sugar. If you need to make it softer, then add milk. Spread over baked cake.

Sidbury Young Farmers and Their Walk to London

Our local Young Farmers are extremely charitably minded and during the year 1990 they made the Slade Centre for handicapped children their Charity of the Year. One of their ideas was to emulate Dick Whittington's walk to London to meet the Lord Mayor. As the Slade Centre was to be the recipient of the funds raised we were fortunate to be invited to take part in the discussions on how the event was to be organized and to have the opportunity of seeing them off, and of welcoming them in London.

They certainly went about it the right way. An enormous cat was made which was placed on a trolley, and a team of Young Farmers dressed in period clothes for the occasion. They set off following a church service at Sidbury on Sunday, May 20th. By coincidence, a friend of mine for many years, Richard Whittington, who lives in Ottery St Mary, is a direct descendant of the famous man; with a little pressure, he agreed to see them off from Sidbury. The picture here gives some idea of their send-off – cheered on their way by supporters and the town band.

It's a long way from Sidmouth to London and by the time the team got to the Guildhall, they were, to put it mildly, exhausted. We were amazed at the wonderful reception given to us by the Lord Mayor of London, Sir Hugh Bidwell, the Lady Mayoress, Mr Sheriff Derek Edwards and his wife, and the Duty Household Officer Colonel J.C.M. Ansell, who duly met the triumphant team who had collected up to £3,000 on the journey. The President of the Young Farmers Club, Peter Ikin, who is also our Senior Vet, and who had kept a fatherly eye on all the proceedings, was there to introduce everybody to the Lord Mayor and the fact that the weather was so perfect made the whole project not only worthwhile but a happy, cheerful event for all.

The start of the walk.

116

Just Some of Our Wonderful Supporters

From Mr and Mrs Paine:

We first arranged to have a stall on the Cathedral Green during the Children's Dance Festival (2,000 children). We bought new and old dolls and I knitted clothes and dressed them, also knitted jumpers, cardigans, etc. We also sold books, second-hand clothes and anything we could get hold of. This was our first attempt and we stood all day in the sun for £34. Rather a failure, we thought. This we followed with your Fiesta at the Sanctuary which was a good day, raising approximately £115.

After that we started indoor and outdoor markets – hard work at £5 a time for the rental of the stall, and sometimes three times a week. We also started craft sales, for which we knitted loads of garments and I got Sid busy knitting gloves and mittens. I made lots of baby bootees, they sold well, but only at 75p a pair. During the outdoor market times we stood in some wicked weather, wind, rain, snow and thunder-storms and we were not allowed to leave until 4 p.m., when all the other marketeers packed up. From 8.30 a.m. this was a long day, and so we decided to finish that stint.

Then we decided to try car boot sales at £3 a time. We travelled all over the place, but if the weather was bad we didn't go, and if it turned out bad when we were there, then we could pack up and come home.

Several empty shops came along in Wells and we pestered estate agents for the loan of one for a few weeks. Apparently only the big name charities could have them, and spend people's money gutting them all out and doing them up posh, which made us mad.

Then our luck changed for a short time when Sid's cousin, Mrs Betty Holland, and her husband let us have a small shop for a couple of months and made no charge for it. When that came to an end we went back to car boot sales. A friend of ours had a wool shop and she was selling off old stock. When she knew what we were doing for the animals she offered it to us and we took a huge load for £200 (nearly had a fit when she said the price). Some we sold as half price packs and we knitted orders for quite a few people. We got our £200 back, with some more added, which we paid to you for your donkeys.

After a while Betty and Leslie Holland came up with another shop and they were going to join in and help us, offering help to other animals and so we introduced Heaven's Gate A.R.C., Redwings Horse and Donkey Sanctuary and as always your huge family. Out of our takings we had to pay towards lights and heating.

Everything went well for a while and loads of goods were brought in to us, then it dwindled down and in the end it was a waste of time staying there, so we closed. And, at seventy years of age, we have now retired. I think we deserve a rest, don't you?

It's nice to know you appreciate the work we have done, and that we have helped you a bit. The money raised in the sale of Christmas cards and books was kept separate and handed over to you. We shall still be helping you as best we can and we wish you great success with your new book.

From Betty Matthews:
For the past seven years, myself and my husband have been fund-raising for this cause by holding jumble sales, etc, and they have certainly been the happiest seven years of my life! Apart from the feeling that we are helping in a small way, we have had such fun and made so many friends from these events, and have regular get-togethers and trips to the Sanctuary for our helpers and supporters so that everyone can see how the money raised is used for the sole benefit of the donkeys.

Of course jumble sales can also be hard work! We have often wished we had our own little donkey and cart, as, having no transport, we are regularly seen carrying bags of jumble, bric à brac and sometimes pushing the odd second hand pram back to the hall when the fun of sorting it begins. However, all this is forgotten when the big day arrives, the doors open and the crowd of bargain-hunters flock in and at the end of the day, when you count the takings, your realize how worthwhile it's all been.

To date from our jumble sales, coffee mornings, etc, we have raised almost £5,000, so I'm sure all those who love the donkeys as we do and have some time to spare would get as much pleasure from this form of fund-raising as we have. So why not have a go!

Extract from letter from Mary Hubbard and Ann Heney –
The Marmalade Sisters:
Since our retirement my sister and I have been able to devote more time to one of our interests which – though connected with the care and well-being of donkeys at the Sanctuary – is mainly for the Slade Centre, as we believe the healing in the broadest sense given by the donkeys to children and youngsters is so worthwhile.

Our support takes the form of raising money with the help of our many friends. We are known either as the Marmalade Sisters or the Pumpkin Chutney Sisters – products which we make in large quantities – also for crochet knee rugs and various scented gifts. It is amazing through the year how the money accrues, as it is known we may have gifts in reserve to sell, and someone may need a present.

We do have coffee mornings and luncheons too, and recently we

Even the donkeys get a present at Christmas.

have been asked to give a talk to a local ladies' group on the work of both the Donkey Sanctuary and the Slade Centre.

It is amazing how one's interest can become infectious in the nicest possible way and we receive gifts of materials and trimmings, soft fruits for jam and jelly, also pumpkins for our special chutney; a local shopkeeper lets us purchase the sugar at cost, which proves how generous people can be towards a very worthwhile cause.

Extract from letter from Stan Bellamy:
People in Bristol know my name because of a notice that is placed outside my bungalow asking for bric à brac and between now and next Slade Centre Festival every spare place in the attic and sheds will start to fill up . . .
People will ring to ask, 'Has my husband brought you some curtains?' or 'Have you had a camera brought in?' One lady missed her roller blinds and some plates! If you come down to the Slade Centre Festival and see a rather large person in a straw hat in a wheelchair with no teeth behind four tables piled high with books, records, china, glasses, cups, saucers, etc, then please buy something to help the Slade Centre and the donkeys.

Extract from letter from Julie Martin (aged 10):
I raised £20 doing a garden fete in our front garden with my friend, Sophie. I had darts, lucky dip, catch-a-fish and books and toy stalls and horseshoes and refreshments, it was great fun! I asked passers-by too, if they didn't want to buy anything, to put their money in a blue box! So, here it is. Good luck with the donkeys.

Bill Cooper, a former industrial engineer living in Tuckenhay, near Totnes, writes:
Since retiring I have given over 50 illustrated talks on four subjects to 25 organizations in 12 towns and villages across South Devon. I do not ask a fee but if offered my expenses I decline and suggest a donation to a favourite charity. In the case of three of the talks the designated recipient is the Donkey Sanctuary. I know for a fact that the mention of "donkeys" has produced a larger than usual donation from some of the organizations involved.

Added to the satisfaction I obtain from giving talks on past experiences is the pleasure gained from knowing that I am also helping the donkeys.

My wife and I interest friends overseas in the work of the Sanctuary. This often results in our sending donations on their behalf, thus easing the transfer of overseas funds.

My wife arouses the interest of lady friends, often house-bound and/or animal lovers, who then knit or crochet items for sale at Sanctuary functions.

The reason for all the fund-raising.

Humphrey, Hugo and the Donkeys

It all began with Humphrey. Humphrey is my 1950s jointed teddy bear. He is 5 inches tall and sits on my shelves at all the Antiques Fairs where I take a stand. One of my customers decided that he (Humphrey) was lonely and presented me with Hugo, who is also jointed but is only 3 inches tall. Hugo, however, is brand new. In spite of this he was very much admired and, as I was always being asked to sell him, this gave me the idea that, if I could get a few 'Hugos' at wholesale price, I could raise some profit to donate to a charity. A few enquiries later I emerged from the shop where Hugo had been purchased in the first place, with some teddies at discount price. Some teddies, in fact, were seven dozen. I spent the rest of that day thinking I must be mad. What on earth could I actually do with 84 teddies?

The next day, Thursday, I set up my stand at the Antiques Fair at Bingley Hall, Stafford Showground. On a small table I placed a

small basket of 'Hugos', with a notice to the effect that the profit from sales of teddies would go to the Donkey Sanctuary, Sidmouth, Devon, and my collecting box. I then crossed my fingers very firmly. On the Friday morning the Fair opened to the general public and on the Saturday morning, on my way back to Stafford to my stand, I made a detour to the shop to buy another seven dozen. I had almost sold out. In fact I sold 69 dozen 'Hugos' before supplies ran out. After a few more Fairs I was being asked for different sizes of teddies and so the whole original idea expanded and over the last two years the teddies have raised over £700 in total. Thanks must also go to my husband, Harry, who puts up with what often looks like a teddy bears' picnic in the kitchen and/or living room of our home and to the organizers of the Antiques Fairs who allow me to set up my charity table. Namely these are Elizabeth Bowman who organizes the Bingley Hall Fair, Shirley Keeling for allowing them at Mansfield Civic Centre and Elvaston Castle, Geoff Whittaker at Newark and last, but by no means least, Anne Stroud who gives me the space and permission at the Shepton Mallet Fair.

Pat Downey

The donkey's dream, by Henry Phillips.

A Most Charming Character!

Just recently I had the most unique and unusual experience, which has been of the greatest benefit to the Donkey Sanctuary. It started with a telephone call from a Major John Millet-Smith. Nothing unusual in that, you may say, but read on!

He asked, in the most educated voice, that I meet him as soon as possible at the Savoy Hotel in London to discuss a large legacy which he wished to leave to the Donkey Sanctuary, adding that he only had a very short time to live. We had a long conversation, as he took pains to tell me of the many happy hours he and his wife had spent petting the donkeys at the Sanctuary in Devon. To quote from the letter which followed: 'My late adored wife and I spent *many, many hours*, indeed, every evening of our holidays making much of the occupants of the Sanctuary. The recent TV "Songs of Praise" was indeed instrumental in shaping my purpose. After 30 years of wonderful life together, I find myself a 63-year-old widower, end of a line, and whose sole companion "hound, Wicklow" will accompany my "last posting" aided by pipes and drums of the Irish Guards! This ceremonial would likely be in the later part of this year, or early next. I do not know exactly when; obviously that is a matter for our Creator and in Wicklow's case, myself.'

Seven years previously, Major Millett-Smith had rescued Wicklow, a cross collie/Alsatian from the Dogs Home, Battersea, aged ten months. He was found swimming off the Orkney Islands, having been dumped off a boat.

We arranged to meet at the Savoy Hotel on Wednesday, July 11th, at 11 a.m., and he sent me a wonderful photograph of himself and Wicklow so that I could recognize him.

I duly arrived at the Savoy Hotel and waited for his arrival in the large lounge below the foyer. I ignored two messages for 'The Lady Elizabeth to contact reception' and it was only when I went to enquire if there had been any message from a Major Millett-Smith that I realized 'The Lady Elizabeth' referred to me! I put them right, and received the message that the Major had been delayed but would be with me by 12 noon. Once again I settled down to wait, but my attention was drawn to a commotion in the main foyer. I wandered up, to be greeted by the strangest sight. It consisted of two immaculate managers trying to restrain an irate Major, with a dog larger than any of them, intent on entering the sacred dog-free premises of the Savoy Hotel.

The Major eyed me above the melee, shouting, 'The Lady

A most charming character.

Elisabeth will allow the dog in. She is an animal lover, and my friend Elizabeth Taylor came in here with her *five* dogs, and you allowed that!' It was my first meeting with the eccentric Major, and certainly not one to be forgotten.

'Lady Elisabeth,' said the desperate manager, 'we cannot allow the dog in. Please ask the Major to leave quietly with his dog.'

'I'm not a Lady,' I said, as I looked hopefully at the Major and beckoned him towards the door. But my pleas were also ignored, and within moments we were all being propelled ignominiously out of the foyer.

'The last time I was here it was as a guest at The Woman of the Year Luncheon,' I mumbled as we were hustled out. It was the first time I had ever been thrown out of anywhere, but I suppose it was an exceptionally high class place to be thrown out of.

We gathered ourselves together, and I untwined Wicklow's lead from the Major's legs, doing my best to stop the dog's constant efforts to kiss me, the Major, and the immaculate but angry managers, who retreated as rapidly as possible into the now quiet majestic premises.

The Major was obviously under the influence of medication and was very unsteady on his feet as we lurched down the Strand. Fortunately there was a welcoming bar just round the corner where they didn't object to dogs, and we gratefully took the last vacant table, trying to recover our morale! With Wicklow happily and noisily gulping a pint mug of water, the Major got us both a drink and told me his wonderful and interesting life story. What a fascinating life he'd had.

He had joined the Irish Guards at 16, by lying about his age, and re-joined when he was old enough. Apart from his Sandhurst training and army life, he had also featured in films with Errol Flynn. His life story was laced with humorous anecdotes but it was obvious he still grieved terribly for his wife, and was fully prepared for his death. His big worry was Wicklow, and I found myself promising to look after him, as I couldn't bear to let that beautiful dog be cremated and buried with him.

When I promised I'd take care of Wicklow, the Major held my hand and said, 'I want you to take a personal gift. My wife owned many diamond rings and I loved to see her wearing them. I want you to promise you'll keep this for yourself.'

I realized he was holding something in his other hand. 'It's really sweet of you,' I said, 'but I can't accept any gifts like that. I never have, it wouldn't be right.'

'But you *will* accept this' he said, his eyes blazing, and he made me open the hand he was holding, pressing something into my palm. It didn't feel like a ring, and when I looked I was amazed to find a little tin soldier dressed in the Irish Guards uniform! Of course I could accept that, and will always treasure it.

The Major told me he wanted the donkeys to have the residue of his Estate, and particularly asked that I attend his special funeral, and that I take Wicklow as soon as he died. He gave me the name of his solicitors, and very sadly I saw him into a taxi with Wicklow (not without some difficulty) and waved goodbye. I had the feeling I would not see him alive again.

I rang the Major's telephone number constantly the following day to ensure his safe return home, but there was no reply, but on my ansaphone that night was the message that he'd had a serious accident and was in a military hospital, and would I come up to see him. I spoke to him the following morning, and to my surprise, he said he had discharged himself and would be returning home.

I rang his solicitors, who were really nice. They too were very concerned about him, and gave me the number of the Social Services with the name of the person looking after his area. The Social Services promised to visit the Major and had obviously been closely concerned with his welfare.

The Major phoned me on numerous occasions over the next two months, and indeed, on our last phone call, he said he'd decided to come and live with me in Sidmouth; he was by then very ill, and my heart ached for him and Wicklow. I'm not sure of the feelings of the other residents of the block of flats in which he lived, as he used to let Wicklow out for a run at all hours of the day and night, recalling him with his bugle!

The Major died during the night of Monday, September 17th. His cousin Victor was with him. He left the fullest instructions for his funeral.

Wicklow was taken into care by his good friend, Andrew Turner, but he was soon desperately ringing for help, as an untrained Wicklow and a small daughter were not compatible. Wicklow arrived under escort at Honiton Station on the 3.10 p.m. train from Waterloo. It was lovely to see him again, and he went straight to John and Monica Fry, who run our large farm in Dorset. They have two spaniels and a collie, and Wicklow, running free with his new friend over the two hundred acres, has decided he is in heaven! John says he hasn't been a second's trouble; 'When I whistle for my collie, Wicklow comes too, they're never apart,' so for Wicklow all ended well!

As for the Major, all I can say is that his funeral was a triumph. From Mary Walker, his solicitor, who made sure every wish was carried out, Canon David Jackson who conducted the service in the most outstanding and personal way, and the undertakers, Frederick Paine, who dressed him as instructed in his officer's uniform plus medals and photographs and placed his sword with a faded red rose (which obviously had immense personal memories)

through the handle, to the Royal Military School of Music who provided a drummer/bugler, all did their bit extremely well.

The instructions for the funeral read as follows:

The drummer/bugler will attend at the church door, to await the arrival of the coffin, then lead the procession up the aisle. When the coffin is in place he will render the Drum Salute to a standing congregation and then join the choir.

The service will then proceed according to the Book of Common Prayer 1662. The three hymns will be accompanied by the drummer/bugler on his kettle drum. The first will be the Irish Refrain 'The Minstrel Boy to the wars hath gone' (two verses, accompanied by the organ in addition to the kettle drum). The second hymn will be the Battle Hymn of the Republic. The third hymn will be 'Amazing Grace'.

After the church service, the coffin, with the sword and rose still in place on top, will be taken to the crematorium, and I wish the drummer/bugler to attend at the crematorium and sound 'The Last Post' as the coffin is taken from view. I would like the hymn 'For those in Peril on the Sea' to be sung.

It was a wonderful end to an incredible man; a man who was different. As the Canon said, he was someone who made an impact on all who met him, and the world was a better place for his being here. We sang his chosen hymns with gusto, the roll of the drums was a triumph, and as the coffin with its sword and entwined rose slowly sunk out of sight at the crematorium, the notes of 'The Last Post' rang out, and in the reverent silence that fell, I knew I was not the only one to be shedding a tear.

Major John Millett-Smith's name will live on – a special plaque will be placed at the Sanctuary in his memory and in grateful thanks for the help he has given to our charity.

Crafts

Many people throughout the country help the Donkey Sanctuary by making different products and selling them for us, and we thought it might be interesting to include in this section some of the ideas and things which people make and how they make them, and perhaps some ideas that you might be able to use at some stage if you feel so inclined.

Elspeth and Mo, two of our most faithful supporters, and a version of the 'I Love Donkeys' jersey.

I Love Donkeys Jumper

Any knitting pattern can be used for the jumper providing the pattern is worked over 54 stitches and it can be made in any ply wool.

Odd rows knit and even rows purl.

Mo Flenley

Knitting pattern for 'I Love Donkeys': this design covers 18 rows and 54 stitches. Knit odd rows plain, even rows purl.

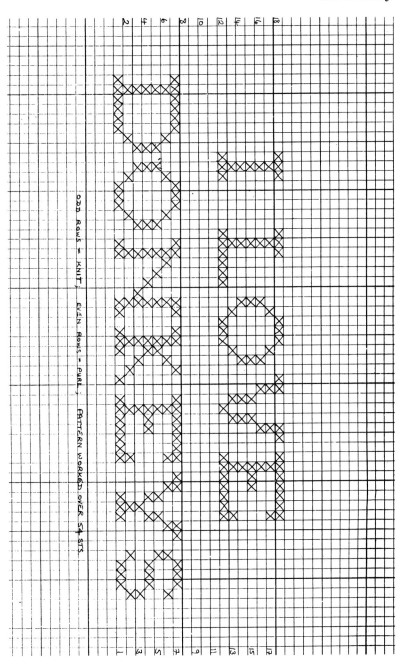

Appliqué

Here is a simple appliqué of a donkey's head, which I designed and made to put on my Sanctuary 'Donkey Week' sweatshirt. It could be used on various garments for adults or children; also for wall hangings, cushion centre panel, pram or cot covers, etc. The amount of times the article will be washed will govern your choice of appliqué fabrics. Always wash a small piece of each fabric to check for colour-run or shrinkage.

If you need to use 'risky' fabrics, it's best to appliqué them to a background fabric which can be hand sewn, like a patch, and easily removed from the garment if need be. I recommend that beginners use this method, particularly if the garment is of stretchy material, e.g. sweatshirt, T-shirt.

The illustrated head is of fur fabric; as most donkeys seem to have white muzzles, I used white felt for that area, but the head could be made all in one colour, which would be even easier to make.

Sylvia – another faithful supporter – and an appliqué donkey.

Pattern for appliqué donkey.
This can be used same size.

Materials

Fur fabric 25 cm × 25 cm
White felt 10 cm × 10 cm
Matching threads for above, for machine stitching
Safety toy eye 10 mm diameter OR domed button on stem
Fabric paints OR dark embroidery thread
Light-weight Vilene 25 cm × 25 cm

Method:

1. On paper, trace the whole design, including all detail such as eye, dotted line around muzzle, zig-zag line of jaw. Use this tracing as a guide when placing appliqué pieces onto background fabric.

2. Place Vilene, shiny side up, onto the design and trace again, as above. If making a white muzzle, end the head tracing at the dotted line. Trace muzzle separately onto Vilene, leaving 5 mm above the dotted line, as this will lie under the main part of nose.

3. With sharp scissors, cut around the outlines (solid lines) and iron the pieces onto the wrong side of the appliqué fabrics.

4. Cut out the pieces, following the outline of the Vilene and taking care not to cut away the underlap allowance.

5. Now assemble the pieces on your background. The white muzzle will be stitched first and you can check its position by laying your first paper tracing over it, after pinning the muzzle in place. Tack around the edge of this piece in white thread, so that your machine stitching will cover the tacking.

6. Using swing needle at its widest setting and very short stitch length (0-1), satin stitch all round the edge, taking care to leave no raw edges. Hold the background fabric firmly while stitching, to prevent puckering.

7. Position main part of head, being sure to overlap at muzzle; check with paper tracing and then tack close to edge with matching thread. Then stitch as in step 6. Do not try to stitch right round 'in one go'. Best to start across the muzzle join, go up one side of head and round ear. Fasten off and start again from other side of muzzle, going round neck edges on solid line and finishing across centre head. The jaw line is shown as a zig-zag line. Stitch along it in satin stitch, starting wide at base and tapering near eye.

8. Trace the oval eye outline and cut the shape in white (or brown) felt. It is not backed with Vilene. Push the toy eye stem through the felt (if using safety eye, do not fix washer yet). Mark correct position for eye on head and cut a small slit through all layers of fabric. Push stem of eye through and attach washer, or sew button firmly in place. Draw in nostrils and mouth, following instruction on fabric paints, or embroider with dark thread.

9. Trim background material to desired shape. It usually looks best to follow a rough outline of the design, rather than cutting a geometric 'patch'. Neaten either by machine, using satin stitch or 'shell' edge, or neatly by hand. Your work is now ready to attach to any article.

Hand method:

This work could be done by hand but it is difficult to get a good outline if using bulky material like fur fabric, as you must turn in the edge to neaten it. Other fabrics could be used, such as cottons, imitation suede, etc.
Follow steps 1, 2 and 3 but in step 4, when cutting you must leave 5 mm (or 10 mm if the fabric frays) around the edge of each piece to turn in.

Position the pieces as described in step 5, tack in place and then sew on by small running stitches, neat hemming or button-hole stitch. All stitches must be small and very close together to give a good outline.

It is easier to appliqué directly onto stretchy garments by hand than by machine, as hand stitching has more 'give'. However, the 'patch' method may still be preferred by beginners and should always be used if the fabric's washing qualities are doubtful.

Good luck with your appliqué.

Sylvia Horne

Decoupage

Decoupage is a way of decorating boxes, plates or other articles made of porcelain, wood or glass – tables, chairs, trays, boxes, plates, vases, glasses, etc. The idea is to use scrap pictures and then seal them with varnish. Wooden items should first be finely sanded and painted or stained before applying the decoupage. If using old wood this should be stripped before sanding. Before painting the wood should be sealed or, if the wood is stained, it should be sealed when dry afterwards.

Spend time arranging the pieces you have cut out and wish to use on the article using Blu-Tack, or similar, to hold temporarily in place. When you are happy with the design, apply glue to the back of the cut-outs. A PVA adhesive should be used on wood and an acrylic adhesive on glass or porcelain.

Place the cut-out in position, cover with a soft absorbent cloth and flatten it with a rubber roller to expel air bubbles and excess glue. Smooth down the edges of the cut-outs with the back of a spoon covered in a cloth.

On wooden items approximately twenty coats of clear varnish will be required until you can no longer feel the edge of the cut-outs. Allow two hours drying time between coats using polyurethane varnish and sand lightly between coats.

Wax and polish the finished article.

Decorating a glass plate:

Draw the circumference of the plate on a piece of paper and arrange the cut-outs on this until you are happy with the design.

Place the plate on top of the design and make the positions of the cut-outs with a crayon.

Apply acrylic adhesive on the bottom of the plate. Lay cut-outs on to the adhesive, checking they line up with the crayon markings. Press out any bubbles with a damp cloth. When dry apply a background film of acrylic water-base paint using a small sponge. After 24 hours apply a further coat and finally two coats of polyurethane varnish.

Children's Donkey Chairs

The design originated from our supporters Mr and Mrs Harvey and, on seeing a donkey chair in the office, our part-time employee Fred Lang thought he would try his hand at making one. This was four years ago and since then, as a hobby, he has produced over 130. They sell for approximately £20 each, and there is never any problem with selling them to raise funds.

The outlay for materials is minimal as the majority of the wood Fred begs from the scrap heap at the timber merchants! Any type of wood can be used.

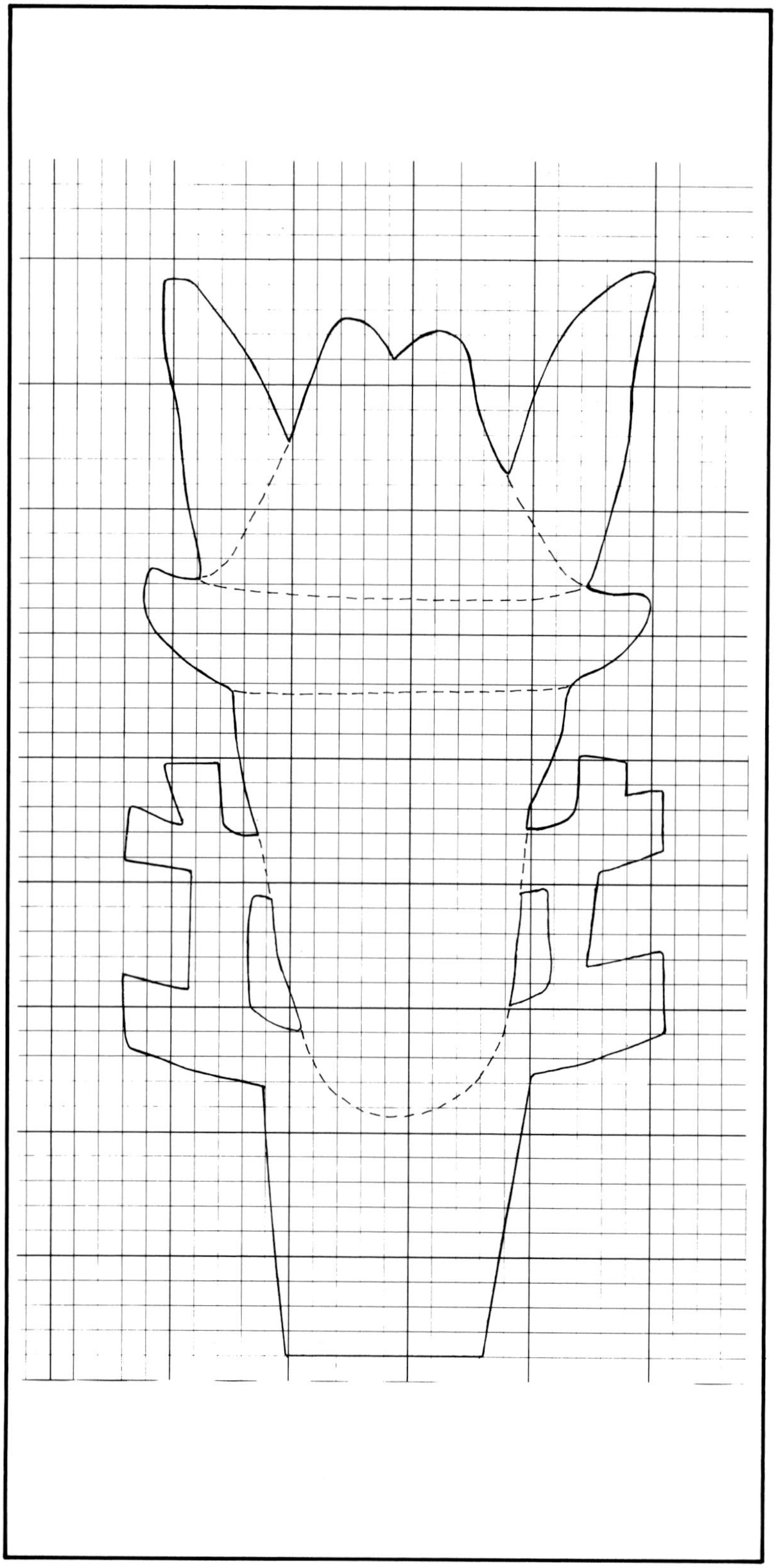

Template for the chair: this has been reduced to one-third, so you should enlarge it by three times.

Approximate measurements:

Overall height of stool 2 ft 2 in/66 cm
Diameter of seat 8 in/20 cm
Height of legs 11 in/28 cm
Thickness of seat 1½ in/4 cm
Thickness of legs 1 in/2½ cm

A template is used for the back of the stool and the wood is cut with a jigsaw. To make the pattern for the seat a colander was initially used for the circle and a straight edge cut at the back (rather like a toilet seat!). The legs are turned on a lathe.

The wood is sanded down. The seat is drilled for the fitting of the legs and the legs glued. A mortice and tenon joint is made where the back of the chair fits into the seat which is pinned and glued.

Mr Alan Goodman, a friend of Fred's, paints the donkey heads. Acrylic paints are used. The remainder of the stool is polished and the whole is then varnished with polyurethane.

Brooch and Badge

The brooch is made from modelling clay which can be purchased from your local craft shop and is sold in various colours. Depending on the size of your donkey brooch two or three donkeys can be made from one small packet of modelling clay.

The clay is extremely pliable and easy to work with once you have kneaded it for a short while. Cut the outline with a pointed knife and mould the body and head with your fingers. Lightly inscribe the eyes, nostrils and hair of the mane and tail.

Bake in the oven to harden the clay. The instructions on the packet of your modelling clay should advise you of temperature and time.

When cold, paint as required with enamel or acrylic paint. The eyes, nostrils, mouth, hoofs, mane and tail of the donkey are lightly painted using an acrylic paint.

Finally a brooch clasp (obtainable from craft shops) should be glued to the back of the brooch using Superglue.

The badge is made from three-ply wood. Trace donkey and mark with pencil on the wood. Cut outline carefully with a fretsaw and then sandpaper lightly ensuring all edges are smooth.

The donkey can either be painted and then varnished or just varnished. A clear polyurethane varnish should be used.

Finally glue a brooch pin to the back of the donkey, using Superglue.

Collage

Firstly start collecting materials and objects for your collage picture. Collage can be made from any material – fabric, wood, paper, etc – and can include photographs, newspaper, tissue paper, hessian, canvas, felt, denim, velvet, blankets, string, rope, wool, dried leaves, etc. The materials need not be new.

Glue appropriate to your chosen fabric must be used, for example, wallpaper paste is suitable for paper and PVA glue for fabric. The background board can be either plywood, hardboard or chipboard which can be covered with canvas or hessian for a good surface on which to work.

After cutting out your donkeys and background items, arrange them on the covered board until you are happy with the display. Glue larger fabric sections first; smaller fabric sections can be glued on top. Apply adequate glue for larger heavier pieces of fabric and use sparingly for items like string.

If the finished picture is framed this does prolong its life and protects it from dust.

A large collage made by the children of Newtown School.

Toy Donkeys

Materials (for a grey donkey – 20 in high):

¾ yd (68 cm) of grey fur fabric
Small piece of white fur fabric for nose and muzzle
Small piece of long fur fabric in dark grey
Square of grey felt for ear lining
Scraps of black felt for hooves and nostrils
Two 10 cm safety eyes
Stuffing (terylene stuffing is best)

Cutting out pattern:

Pin all pattern pieces to wrong side of fur fabric, ensuring pile is running smooth to lower edge. Place pattern pieces with arrows running in same direction.

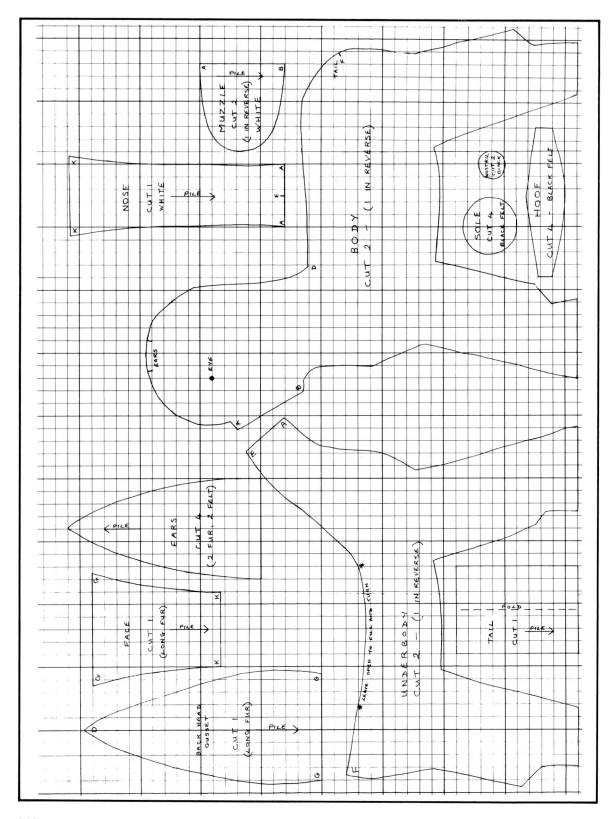

MUZZLE
CUT 2
(1 IN REVERSE)
WHITE

NOSE
CUT 1
WHITE
PILE →

BODY
CUT 2 — (1 IN REVERSE)

TAIL
F

SOLE
CUT 4
BLACK FELT

NOSTRIL
CUT 2
BLACK

HOOF
CUT 4 — BLACK FELT

EARS
EYE

EARS
CUT 4
(2 FUR, 2 FELT)
← PILE

FACE
CUT 1
(LONG FUR)
PILE →

BACK HEAD
GUSSET
CUT 1
(LONG FUR)
PILE →

UNDERBODY
CUT 2 — (1 IN REVERSE)
LEAVE OPEN TO FILL AND TURN

TAIL
CUT 1
FOLD
PILE →

140

Cut through backing of fabric only with sharp scissors.

Oversew all edges by hand to stop the fur slipping.

Seam allowance is ¼ in for machine or hand sewing.

To make up pattern:

1. With right sides facing join underbody from E to F leaving opening for turning and stuffing.
2. Join face to nose and back head gusset, matching letters.
3. Mark eyes in head with thread.
4. Join muzzle to side of head A to B.
5. Join nose A to E to A to underbody A to E to A.
6. Join main body to underbody sewing from A round legs to F.
7. Join face, nose and head gusset to head, easing round muzzle.
8. Stitch A to D. Insert one eye.
9. Repeat from other side of body. Insert other eye.
10. Continue stitching D to F.
11. Turn and stuff firmly. Sew opening with ladder stitch.
12. Release fur from seams with eye of needle or teazle brush.

To make ears:

Join felt to fur fabric.

Sew on wrong side leaving bottom edges open.

Turn ears to right side. Fold sides together. Catch bottom edges together. Lightly sew to top of head.

To make tail:

Fold right sides together and sew down side.

Turn tail to right side, making sure seam edge comes down the centre of the tail at the back.

Catch edges together at the bottom of the tail.

Stuff tail lightly and then catch edges at top of tail.

Sew in place on donkey back.

To make hooves and nostrils:

Join short sides of hoof together making a circle. Insert sole. Make four.

Slip over bottom of leg and stitch in place.

Cut 2 circles of black felt the size of a 1p coin. Glue in place on nose for nostrils.

Ladder stitches:

If legs splay outwards, ladder stitches from the top of the inside leg into the underbody and pulled tightly will bring the legs straight and allow donkey to stand up.

Mrs Dorothy Ward

The real thing.

Atha Donkey

Miss U. Westell has for many, many years made 'Animal Toys to Help Animals' (ATHA) and has kindly supplied us with the pattern and instructions for making the ATHA donkey which is 12 in high and made in fur fabric and felt. Six donkeys can be made from one metre of fur fabric. (Wire is used in the making, so perhaps these donkeys are not suitable for very young children.)

Materials

¼ metre of fur fabric
felt in toning colour to fur fabric for tail, mane, hoofs, nostrils, eyes, soles and ears (or ears can be made completely of fur fabric)
brown felt for pannier and saddlebag
small scraps of coloured felt for flowers and small scraps of white, black and brown or blue for eyes
green wool for flower stems
2½ metres fine agricultural wire for leg supports
scraps of cloth for winding around wire leg supports
white tape ⎱
piping cord ⎰ for halter

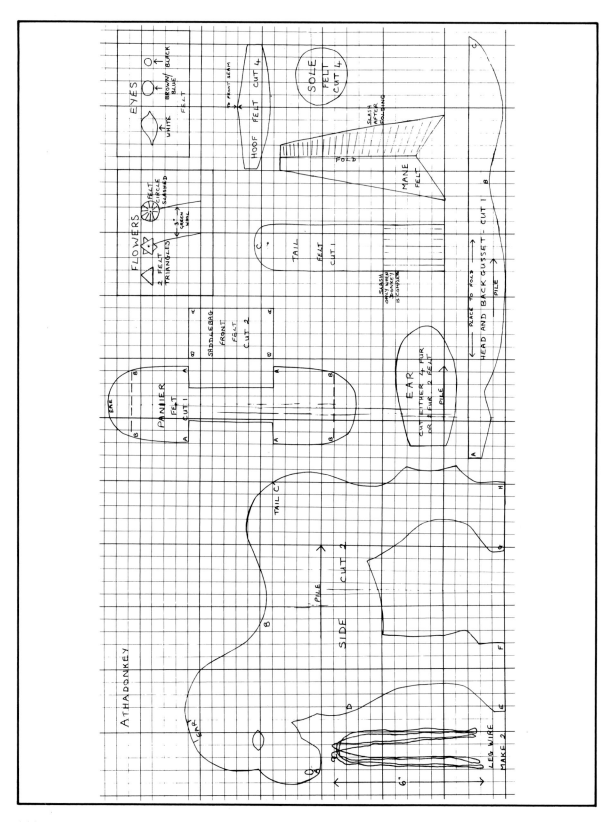

Instructions:

Stick paper pattern onto stiff card and cut out with a sharp knife or scissors. Place fur fabric wrong side up with pile running from left to right. Lay templates on material and draw round each piece with pencil or tailor's chalk. Reverse pieces so that the paired parts provide mirror-images of the first and, where a fold is indicated, provide the other side of the fold. Cut out with sharp scissors and tack together.

Ears: make these either by joining two pieces of fur fabric round curved edges, leaving base open, or by sticking felt pieces accurately to fur fabric pieces and, when dry, trimming round edges. Fold in half and stitch base to top of head where indicated.

Eyes: assemble eyes, or use glass safety eyes, inserting where indicated before assembling donkey.

Tail: roll up sideways and stitch or stick edge firmly as far as fringe.

Body, head, legs: tack parts of donkey together, including base of tail at C. Match curves and angles, easing where necessary. Leave gap of 2 in one side of undergusset/side join for stuffing. Machine or sew backstitch. If hand sewing, remember that seams must not gape when stuffed so each stitch must be pulled tight but not puckered. Pay special attention to where ears and tail are included in seams. Turn inside out.

Feet: backstitch soles firmly to open ends of legs.

Stuffing: Now comes the worst part – the stuffing. Wind four lengths of agricultural wire (fine) together to form the strength of the legs. Cover with cloth wound round each. Insert a small pad of cloth into each foot, then place the wires into each leg. With a long, fine knitting needle or a pair of hairdresser's scissors (they have long, fine blades and are better) insert the tiny bits or strips of stuffing right down into the feet, pressing firmly and building up very gradually a hard, strong leg. Stuff head firmly and evenly, moulding all the time, finally, stuff body firmly. This is quite hard work and may need unstuffing and a restart but it is essential that the standing donkey should be firm and not floppy.

When apparently firmly stuffed it is recommended that the donkey be left a few hours or overnight when it will be found that stuffing has 'settled' and will need more added before sewing up with ladder stitch the gap left for stuffing.

Brush well with wire brush, trim the hair short round site of eyes

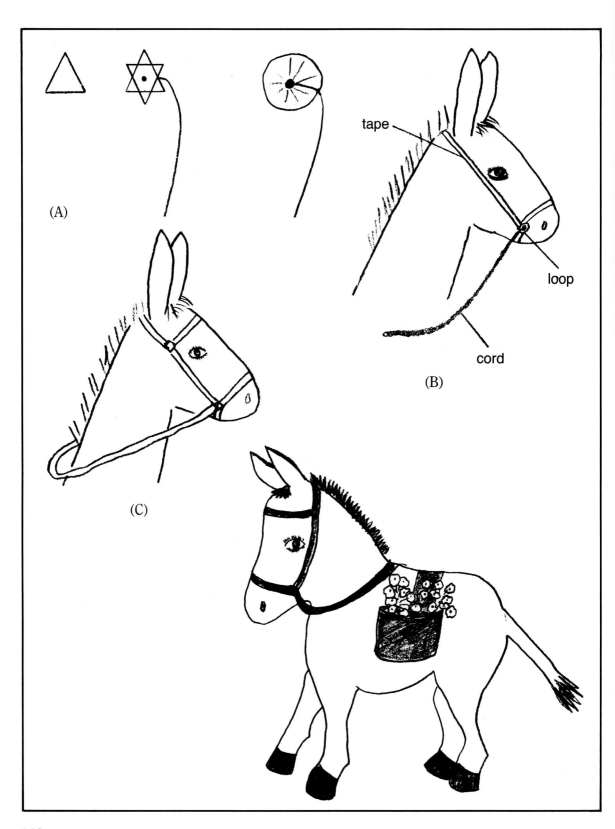

(A)

(B)

tape

loop

cord

(C)

and pin these in position, sticking or stitching firmly when satisfied with placement.

Trim hair short all over nose and stick or stitch nostrils in place. Trim lower legs and stick hoofs in place securing short edges at back with a few stitches.

Optional extras: panniers full of flowers are an attractive addition and flowers can be made from scraps of different coloured felt.

The flowers, whether made from two triangles or a slashed circle, should be pierced by a needle carrying green wool, a large knot of wool forming centre of flower. Another knot is made close behind the flower, securing it from slipping down the stem. (Illustration A)

Stitch the fronts of saddlebags to the wide ends of the pannier, easing the curved end into the edge marked BB. Each saddlebag needs 30-35 flowers to look full and not skimpy. Gather the stems together and bind with green wool. Slip the ends into a pannier and stitch to the back. Secure the pannier to the back and sides of the donkey, making sure bags are level.

Halter: this simple but effective extra is made from white tape and fine piping cord. Measure the tape round from one side of the muzzle over top of head and down to level with the starting end. Stitch a loop both sides large enough to thread the cord through. From the second loop take the tape over the nose, thread it through the first loop and cut off. Wrap the free end round the end of cord as far as possible and stick or stitch in place. Draw the 'rope' across under chin and thread through second loop. Knot end or glue to prevent fraying about 8 in from joint with tape. (Illustration B)

Bridle: alternatively rather than a halter a bridle can be made cutting felt a ¼ in wide and fixing as per illustration. (Illustration C)

Jigsaw

The jigsaw puzzle is made by pasting the Donkey Sanctuary poster onto stiff card, making sure that it is stuck down really well. Leave to dry thoroughly. The cutting edges can then be drawn freehand onto the picture. Cut out carefully with a craft knife, making sure that the card is cut right through.

A more sturdy jigsaw puzzle can be made by using thin plywood instead of card, and cutting out with a fretsaw.

147

Stencilling

This can be used to decorate walls, floors, wooden furniture, fabrics, paper, etc.

Materials

Stencil card   Tracing paper   Masking tape
Craft knife   Carbon Paper   Paint

The stencil card should be slightly larger than the donkey design.

1. Trace the donkey design on tracing paper. Place the tracing on top of the carbon paper on the stencil card and draw the design in the centre. You can use it any size you wish – enlarge or reduce according to preference.

2. Fix the stencil card to a wooden board with masking tape to protect the surface you are resting on.

3. Carefully cut the stencil trying to obtain a bevelled edge in order that the stencil has a neat finish.

4. With masking tape or a spray adhesive that allows for repositioning fix the stencil to the area you are decorating.

Various paints can be used, i.e. water colours, inks, felt tip pens, poster paints on cardboard; oil, enamel, acrylic or vinyl wall paints on most other surfaces.

Children's Corner

Obviously one of the main projects of the Donkey Sanctuary is to educate future generations not only to love and appreciate donkeys, but also to know what a donkey's needs are and to be able to help us by looking out for donkeys in trouble in the UK and abroad whilst on holiday.

We have designed a 'Lesson' which is sent out to schools throughout the country and which we hope will give teachers sufficient information to enable them to develop an interesting project on the donkey. We get help from a lot of schools which, having carried out a donkey project, decide that they will help the Sanctuary and we get many happy visits from groups of schoolchildren delighted to come and see the Sanctuary for themselves.

This section includes the Lesson on the Donkey (perhaps you would like to impart some of this knowledge to children you know?) as well as children's projects, including a few recipes for treats both for donkeys and humans; we hope that both young and old will enjoy this!

'Suey thinks she's in heaven' by Susan Knight, Holmlea School, Glasgow.

For Young Readers

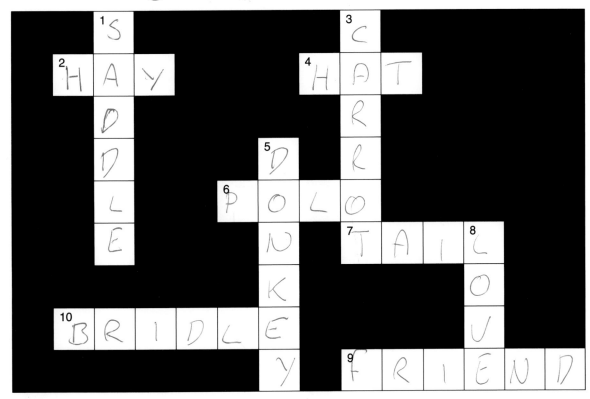

ACROSS

2. Your donkey might eat this in the winter.

4. You wear this on your head when you ride.

6. It's white, round, has a hole in the middle, and donkeys love them.

7. It swishes flies away.

9. A donkey is a _____ for life.

10. Your donkey wears it on its head when being ridden or handled.

DOWN

1. You sit on it when you ride.

3. Long and orange and can be eaten.

5. A _____ is a friend for life.

8. Your donkey will want lots of this.

(Solution on p. 176)

Donkey Breed Society Juniors

Join the dots and find out what the donkey is doing

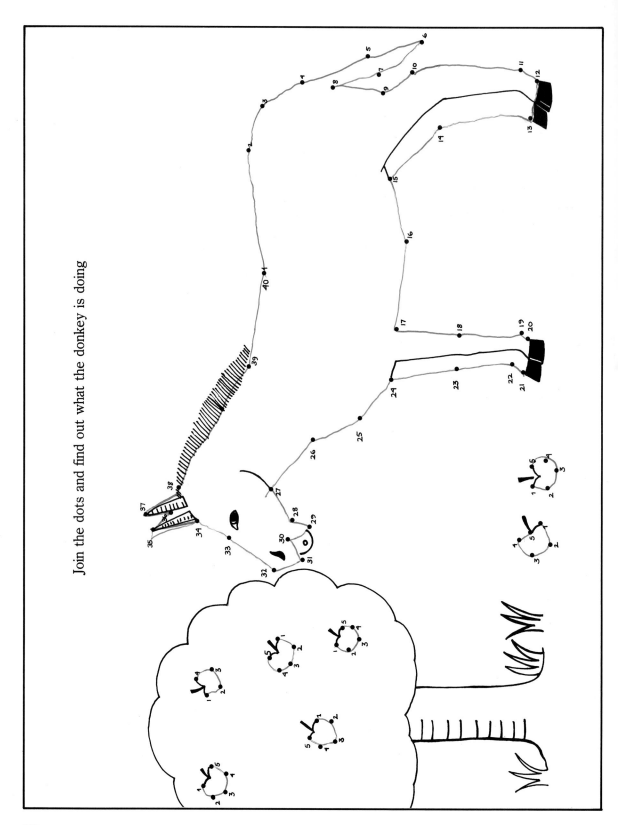

Can you help the donkey
to find the carrot?

Donkey Talk

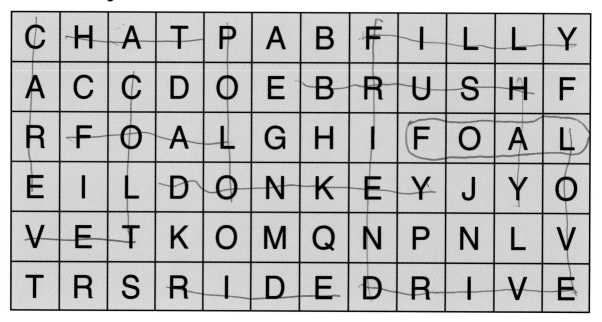

C	H	A	T	P	A	B	F	I	L	L	Y
A	C	C	D	O	E	B	R	U	S	H	F
R	F	O	A	L	G	H	I	F	O	A	L
E	I	L	D	O	N	K	E	Y	J	Y	O
V	E	T	K	O	M	Q	N	P	N	L	V
T	R	S	R	I	D	E	D	R	I	V	E

Foal   Colt   Polo   Care   Hat   Drive   Love   Vet

Donkey   Filly   Ride   Brush   Friend   Hay

Find these words in the grid and ring or put a line through them. Which one appears twice?

Foal

(Answer on p. 176)

Donkey Breed Society Juniors

154

Word Search

H	S	U	R	B	Y	D	N	A	D	R	S
S	A	R	S	B	E	B	M	O	U	T	P
U	Z	B	O	O	F	M	I	K	A	S	O
R	P	W	O	D	C	O	J	B	E	A	N
B	O	D	F	Y	U	C	L	K	F	P	G
R	E	S	C	B	R	E	X	C	S	T	E
E	G	J	A	R	R	N	V	I	Q	N	P
T	S	Y	R	U	Y	A	W	P	L	U	G
A	B	R	B	S	C	M	R	F	B	G	I
W	O	B	G	H	O	O	F	O	I	L	N
A	E	R	V	Y	M	P	H	O	O	J	R
R	S	U	A	S	B	T	M	H	M	L	A

Here are a few things you might find in your grooming kit – especially if you are going to a show!

If you use all of these items in the manner described you will have a very well groomed donk, with a shining coat and you will have just spent at least an hour of very hard work! But don't groom your donkey like this every day as some brushes can remove essential oils and grease from the coat, making it even less weather-proof than it is now.

(Answers on p. 176)

Donkey Breed Society Juniors

Know Your Donkey

ACROSS

1. Something a donkey needs everyday.

4. Something you love a lot.

5. Something that your donkey has every day and it is green.

7. This makes them look lovely.

DOWN

2. Something you should clean after you have ridden.

3. An activity you can do with a donkey.

6. A bedding that donkeys sleep on.

(Solution on p. 176)

Georgina Taylor

Donkey Breed Society Juniors

Questions for Young Children

(Answers on p. 176)   *Sue Brennan*

1. What would you catch your donkey with?

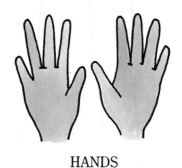

(HALTER)   HANDS   LASSO

2. What sort of bedding would you give your donkey?

MATTRESS   (STRAW)   CARPET

3. What would you give your donkey to drink?

LEMONADE   (WATER)   MILK

4. What would you give your donkey to eat?

HAY   SANDWICHES   LEAVES

5. What would you put on your donkey's back for you to ride in?

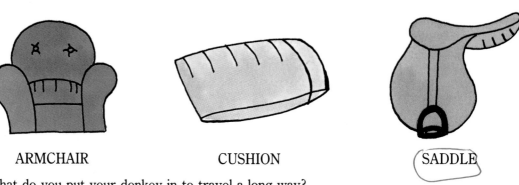

ARMCHAIR   CUSHION   SADDLE

6. What do you put your donkey in to travel a long way?

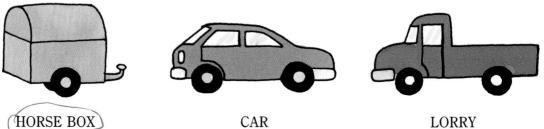

HORSE BOX   CAR   LORRY

7. What would you put your donkey's feed in?

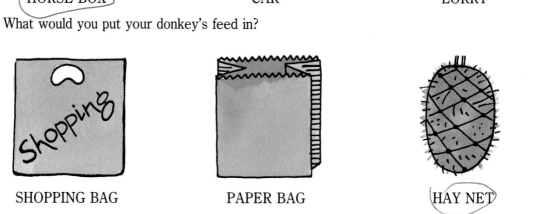

SHOPPING BAG   PAPER BAG   HAY NET

8. What would you use to muck out a stable?

MOP AND BUCKET

FORK

BUCKET AND SPADE

9. What would you clean your donkey's feet with?

TOOTHBRUSH

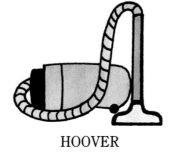

HOOVER

HOOF PICK

10. Which brush would you use to groom your donkey's coat?

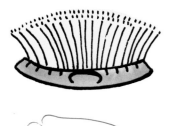

BODY BRUSH

HAIR BRUSH

BROOM

11. Where would your donkey live?

HOUSE

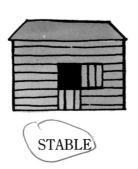

STABLE

CARAVAN

Recipes

Yorkshire Spice Cake – from Mrs Svendsen's Auntie Effie Gowling

2 cups of flour
1 teaspoon salt
1 teaspoon baking powder
1 cup mixed fruit
4 oz (110 g) butter
1 teaspoon mixed spice
½ teaspoon cream of tartar
1 cup sugar
3 eggs
Milk to mix

Mix dry ingredients, rub in fat and add beaten eggs, melted treacle and milk, adding the baking powder and bicarbonate of soda last. Mix well and bake in a moderate oven for about two hours.

Goosnargh Cakes

12 oz (340 g) flour
8 oz (220 g) best butter
4 oz (110 g) caster sugar
½ teaspoon coriander seeds

Work fat into flour with the hand until a paste is formed. Add coriander seeds and 2 oz (55 g) of the sugar. Knead the mixture for about 10 minutes, then turn onto a floured board and roll out to ¼ in (6 mm) thick. Cut with a round cutter and place on a tin covered with greaseproof paper. Put a teaspoon of sugar on each cake and allow to stand overnight. Bake in a slow oven for about 20 minutes. The cakes must not be brown. Cover with caster sugar.

Buffalo Cake

2 cups flour
1 cup sugar
4 oz (110 g) butter
½ cup milk
1 teaspoon bicarbonate of soda
2 teaspoons cream of tartar
2 eggs

Mix all ingredients to a thick batter. Pour into a tin and bake in a hot oven 30-40 minutes. If preferred mix in a few raisins.

Peppermint Creams

1 lb (450 g) icing sugar
Evaporated milk
Icing sugar to dust
¼ teaspoon cream of tartar
Peppermint essence

Sieve icing sugar and cream of tartar. Add enough evaporated milk to make a stiff paste and two drops of peppermint essence. Taste and if not pepperminty enough add another drop of essence. Knead mixture with your hands, adding a little extra icing sugar to stop it being too sticky! With a rolling pin roll the mixture to about ½ inch (1 cm) thick and cut into fancy shapes. With a pastry brush moisten top of the creams with evaporated milk. Place in small paper cases or arrange on a plate. Eat peppermint creams, sharing some with donkey friends if possible.

Oatmeal Parkin – from Mrs Svendsen's Auntie Effie Gowling

8 oz (220 g) medium oatmeal
½ teaspoon salt
1 teaspoon bicarbonate of soda
3 tablespoons treacle
4 oz (110 g) sugar
8 oz (220 g) plain flour
1 teaspoon ground ginger
8 oz (220 g) butter or margarine
2 eggs
Milk to mix

Rub butter into flour and add other dry ingredients. Warm the treacle, add beaten eggs and milk and add to mixture. Beat well, place in baking tin and cook for about one hour at 325°F.

Russian Toffee

1 lb (450 g) sugar
4 oz (110 g) butter
2 tablespoons syrup
1 large tin condensed milk
2 tablespoons water

Melt sugar, butter and syrup in pan. Add milk and water. Boil for 20 minutes, stirring all the time. Test for setting by dropping a small ball of the mixture into a glass of cold water. This should form a soft ball. Then pour into greased tray and when set cut into pieces.

Ginger Biscuits for Donkeys and Humans

8 oz (220 g) flour
2 teaspoons ground ginger
8 oz (220 g) Demerara sugar
4 oz (110 g) butter
1 large egg
1 level teaspoon bicarbonate of soda
1 tablespoon milk

Mix the flour, ginger and sugar together. With your fingers rub the butter into the mixture. Dissolve the soda in the milk. Add the egg to the milk and soda and beat with a wooden spoon. Pour the milk mixture on to the flour mixture. Mix well with your hands. Roll the mixture into balls. Place the balls onto a greased baking tray, well separated, and press each ball once on top. Bake in a moderate oven, 325°F for 30 minutes.

Puzzle Time

Can you unscramble these letters to find twenty things you need to keep, show or ride a donkey?

1. LEDIF — FIELD
2. ASLTEB — STABLE
3. REELTHS — SHELTER
4. WARTS — STRAW
5. TCEBKU — BUCKET
6. NATHYE — HAYNET
7. ADEH LORACL — HEAD COLLAR
8. GANDLIE NERI — LEADING REIN
9. YODB SHRUB — BODY BRUSH
10. NYDDA UHBRS — DANDY BRUSH
11. RURYC MCBO — CURRY COMB
12. FOHO CIPK — HOOF PICK
13. HFOO LOI — HOOF OIL
14. DALESD — SADDLE
15. LIREDB — BRIDLE
16. SENIR — REINS
17. PRISTRUS — STIRRUPS
18. RIGHT — GIRTH
19. PERRUCP — CRUPPER
20. TABLENK — BLANKET

(Answers on p. 176)   *Donkey Breed Society Juniors*

A Lesson on the Donkey

Origins of the Donkey

The donkey's ancestors were wild asses from Africa and Asia. In Africa there were two separate species: the Nubian, standing 12 hands, from the north between the Mediterranean coast and the Sahara Desert; and the Somali, standing 14 hands, from further east to the south of the Red Sea. The Nubian wild ass had a shoulder cross which was not very marked, being either rather short or very thin, but he had no stripes on his legs. In contrast the Somali wild ass had no shoulder cross, but very prominent leg-stripes, reminiscent of the zebra. The regions where they lived were hot and dry, so that there was little difference between the thickness of their winter and summer coats. In winter both were

Feeding time at the Sanctuary.

grey, in summer the Nubian had a reddish tinge and the Somali a yellowish tinge.

The Asiatic branch of the breed came from a much larger area stretching from the Red Sea to northern India and Tibet where the ass had to adapt to differences of climate, terrain and altitude. Consequently there is no single type of Asiatic wild ass. The further east the ass was found, the larger, heavier and stronger the animal became. The Syrian wild ass measured under 10 hands. His neighbour to the east was the light-coloured swift-footed onager, which measured 12 hands. East again was the kulan, standing half a hand higher, darker in colour, with a very marked broad stripe along his back and growing a thick winter coat. Like all Asiatic wild asses, he does not have a shoulder stripe. Then comes the largest and heaviest of all the Asiatic wild asses, the kiang, standing 14 hands, living on the Tibetan plateau to the north of the Himalayas and adapting to extremes of climate. He has certain features more like a horse than our domesticated donkey, such as shorter ears and a rounder foot.

Through all these countries ran the trade route from the Pacific Ocean to the Mediterranean given the romantic name of the Silk Road. The journey lasted several years and no single animal completed the entire journey. Donkeys were among the draught animals used and with unplanned matings, while passing through the territories of the various Asiatic wild asses, some mixing of the breeds occurred. Carrying the valuable bales of silk, the donkeys arrived ultimately in Alexandria. Through Asia Minor donkeys arrived in Greece where they proved to be ideal animals to work on the narrow paths between the vines. Their use in the cultivation of grapes spread through the Mediterranean countries to Spain whose coast, at the southern tip, is separated from North Africa by only a few miles.

With the Roman army the donkey travelled throughout the Roman Empire as a pack animal and later was used in agriculture and in the new vineyards which the Romans planted as far north as France and Germany. With the Roman invasion of Britain, donkeys came to England. For 1,500 years no one bothered about them, as was the case, though for a shorter period, in the twentieth century.

So why did the donkey begin to attract attention and why was he suddenly needed? The answer was war. For hundreds of years the demand for horses as cannon fodder had been difficult to meet. They were either requisitioned by the army or taken in payment of taxes. By the sixteenth century horses had become scarce and expensive. The desperate farmer needed a replacement and in England and Wales the replacement was the neglected donkey. Years later, at the end of the nineteenth century, Welsh-bred

In the Middle Ages, if you had eye trouble, you would smear fresh donkey dung over your eyes!

The cure in ancient times for the sting of a scorpion was for the sufferer to sit upon an ass with his face to the tail or whisper in the animal's ear, 'A scorpion has stung me.' The pain was transferred from the man to the ass but the ceremony had to be performed on a lucky day and at a lucky hour.

The cure for gout was to bind a donkey's hoof on the bad foot.

There is a saying that if you kiss a mule you won't get scarlet fever.

donkeys were much sought after and commanded a high price.

There has been no mention of Ireland which many people think of as the home of the donkey. Once again it was England's wars – this time with the Irish – which brought the donkey to Ireland with the army of occupation. In this country, too, the army began to buy cheap horses required for other wars and the Irish farmers were more than happy to take cash, replace their horses with cheaper donkeys and put the surplus cash under the bed!

In Scotland the donkey has never been so commonly used. Two reasons for this are the cold winters unlike the mild, though damp, climate of Ireland, and Scotland's extensive area of forests, very different from the donkey's original habitat.

Whilst the donkey, particularly the white ass, had some aristocratic and even royal owners, nevertheless in England and Wales he remained the 'poor man's horse'. He was cheap to keep, at least until the end of the eighteenth century, when the Inclosure Acts abolished certain commons rights and deprived commoners of their free grazing. The farmers complained that there was no money in breeding donkeys – a cry to be heard from donkey breeders again!

Breeding mules by crossing a donkey stallion with a horse or pony mare showed more profit. The New Forest in Hampshire was a centre for this activity, since it was near the port of Southampton from which the young mules were shipped to the USA. However, they were small and not of good quality and to produce a bigger animal, the New Forest jackass was replaced as a stallion by the larger Spanish or Maltese ass.

The heyday of the donkey in Britain was during the last century when it was used on farms and increasingly in towns as a pack animal. In Ireland the donkeys carried the peat from the bogs and drew the carts loaded with potatoes or with flax to be woven into Irish linen. In fashionable spas, donkeys transported corpulent ladies to take the waters. On the sands, the donkeys gave rides to young visitors. In the mining areas, it was the coal miners who rode their donkeys to work at the collieries. Donkeys pulled lawnmowers on the lawns of prosperous houses and the rubbish carts of the local councils. They carried the laundry and delivered the milk. In fact, donkeys also supplied the milk! In London a herd of milch-asses made a daily round of some smart residential districts where the donkeys were milked in the street to produce asses' milk for the children of well-to-do families. For the successful tradesman and the London coster-monger the donkey barrow came to replace the baskets and the handcarts. Hundreds of donkeys were drawn up at the markets for the carts to be filled with fresh fruit, vegetables and fish and on bank holidays the donkey would be used to take the family for an outing.

Donkeys Abroad

Donkeys are generally used to carry loads through rough country where there are no roads, between villages, up steep narrow mountain paths where lorries cannot go, and through desert lands. Donkeys travel about 2.5 miles per hour (approximately 4 kilometres) and in most countries average 15 miles (24 kilometres) per day. In many countries they are also used in agriculture to plough and till the land. Through our separate charity, the International Donkey Protection Trust, we help these donkeys in many ways by improving conditions, educating the owners and treating the donkeys for parasites (worms in their stomachs).

In Lamu, an island off the coast of Kenya, we have set up a sanctuary. It has a surgical treatment room and intensive care boxes. The sanctuary arranges daily feeding for the starving donkeys found wandering in the town, provides long-term care for orphaned foals and the very sick, holds daily clinics to treat wounds, etc, worms all donkeys on Lamu and the surrounding islands and has commenced a tetanus inoculation programme. A trough outside the sanctuary provides water for all passing donkeys. On this particular island there are approximately 3,850 donkeys and as there are no vehicles on the island, except the Land Rover belonging to the Chief Commissioner, the donkeys do all the work and carry heavy loads of coral and mahogany.

On trips to Greece and Turkey some time ago Mrs E. D. Svendsen, Administrator of the International Donkey Protection Trust, found that the average age of donkeys in these countries was under 20 years old – half the life span of donkeys in England. It appeared that the cause could be parasites and we therefore set up a controlled test in Greece which has proved this. However, if the parasites can be controlled the donkeys will then live longer and be healthier and will therefore help the people of these countries, some of whom are extremely poor. The Agricultural Bank of Greece then allocated 150 million drachma (over £1 million) to subsidize anthelmintics (wormer) and included donkeys in this treatment for the first time.

In Mexico, Cyprus, Egypt, Ethiopia and Kenya trials have been set up involving the veterinary universities and ministries. Vets from each of these countries have visited us with the co-operation of the World Health Organization and have benefited from their experience and training given in the UK. It is becoming apparent that more and more interest is being raised in donkey welfare in view of its value as an agricultural animal in the Third World and we have recently been called in to advise in Nigeria and Tanzania.

We are continuing in our efforts to prevent the barbaric cruelty inflicted on a poor donkey each year at a fiesta held at Villanueva de

In Germany many people think it is good luck to eat a green food on the Thursday before Easter. At one time, some people even believed that if they didn't eat a green salad on that day, they would turn into donkeys.

In France during medieval times there were no doctors for the peasants but one of the remedies of the 'wise women' was the breath of an ass to drive poison from the body.

In Ireland when a donkey brays another tinker has passed away.

In Ghana it is the practice to blindfold a donkey before slaughter. Presumably in association with avoiding the 'evil eye' of the donkey at the time of killing it.

166

The corpse of Alexander the Great was carried on a bier pulled by sixty-four mules from Babylon to Alexandria.

Small girl helping donkey owner to gather strawberries in the garden.
'What do you put on your strawberries?'
'Well, we use the donkey dung.'
'Oh, do you? We use cream on ours.'

la Vera, Spain. Blackie, rescued from the village in 1987, is safely in care at the Donkey Sanctuary and will receive care and kindness for the rest of his natural life.

Plans are being made to build a clinic in Ethiopia where donkeys play a vital role in the economy of the country and have survived the droughts better than camels. By providing help to the donkeys and making them fitter and able to live and work longer we hope that we are helping man under the most desperate conditions.

To help combat the terrible problems in Mexico we employ a veterinary surgeon and assistant who travel in our mobile veterinary unit to remote areas around Mexico City, where equine neglect and mistreatment are frequent, providing much needed help to donkeys and mules.

Donkeys in This Country

Many donkeys in this country work too – mainly on the beaches, donkey derbys and at fetes. Until recently there was no law to protect them and they were often as overworked as the donkeys abroad. The donkeys would be driven to the beach early in the morning and give rides to all sizes of children until late in the evening, standing all day in the blazing hot sun. Now donkeys are protected to a certain extent as in almost every part of the country beach operators have to be licensed. This means they are inspected twice yearly by a veterinary surgeon and a member of the local council.

General Facts on Donkeys

Gestation period is ten and a half to fourteen and a half months – no accurate date can be specified as in cattle. Donkeys rarely have twins. The donkey foal stands within minutes of being born and has a full coat of hair. Unlike other animals they do not instinctively know where to find the 'milk bar' and will frequently search for hours before suckling; this could be nature's way of weeding out weak foals. Foals are delicate up to the age of one year, the main dangers being wet and cold. No mare under the age of four should be put in foal, and no donkey under this age should be ridden. Donkeys do not require 'breaking-in' quite so much as the horse and need only very simple training.

Donkeys can live to a very old age – at the Sanctuary we have many over 20 years old and some who are almost 50 years old.

Quiz

1. Do you know what a female donkey is called?

   ✓A. *A mare or a jenny donkey*
   B. *A lady donkey*
   C. *A feline donkey*

2. What is a male donkey called?

   A. *A buck or stag donkey*
   ✓B. *A stallion or a jack donkey*
   C. *A man donkey*

3. What is a mule?

   ✓A. *An animal who has a donkey for a father and a horse for a mother*
   B. *An animal who has a donkey for a mother and a horse for a father*
   C. *An animal whose mother and father cannot breed*

4. What is the maximum age a donkey can live?

   A. *15 yrs*
   B. *30 yrs*
   ✓C. *50 yrs*

5. At what age may a donkey be ridden without causing harm to its back?

   A. *2 yrs*
   ✓B. *4 yrs*
   C. *6 yrs*

6. Approximately how many donkeys are there in the world?

   A. *200,000*
   B. *12,500,000*
   ✓C. *55,000,000*

7. How many times a year should a donkey's hooves be trimmed?

   A. *2 times a year*
   ✓B. *6 times a year*
   C. *10 times a year*

8. How long is a donkey's pregnancy?

   A. *6 months*
   ✓ B. *10½-14½ months*
   ✗C. *18 months*

9. What is the maximum weight a donkey should carry?

   A. *76 kg (12 stone)*
   B. *101 kg (16 stone)*
   ✓C. *50 kg (8 stone)*

10. In which of these countries do donkeys no longer work?

   A. *Ethiopia*
   B. *Mexico*
   C. *England*
   ✓D. *None of the above*

(Answers on p. 176)

Poems and Paintings from Young Contributors

'Eeyore runs off with a visitor's bag' by Jayne Watson, Holmlea School, Glasgow.

Bray, Bray, Bray

Donkey, donkey,
Bray, bray, bray,
Out in the field every day –
Thinking about the things he's done,
Running about like a big loud drum.

Happy donkey, happy day,
If you listen now you hear his bray,
Being happy, being free,
That's all the donkey wants to be.

Sharleen Walker
Donkey Breed Society Juniors

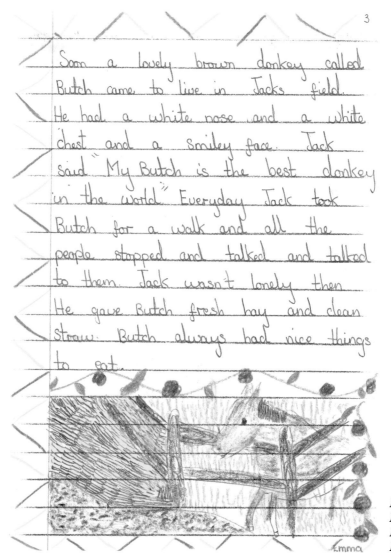

Soon a lovely brown donkey called Butch came to live in Jacks field. He had a white nose and a white chest and a smiley face. Jack said "My Butch is the best donkey in the world." Everyday Jack took Butch for a walk and all the people stopped and talked and talked to them. Jack wasn't lonely then. He gave Butch fresh hay and clean straw. Butch always had nice things to eat.

From 'A Book For Jack' by Honiton Partial Hearing Unit.

'Mother trying to catch Eeyore as he runs off with the carrots' by Kirsty-Ann Wilson, Holmlea School, Glasgow

'He-haw' I love to hear!
How I wish I had, like you, good ears!
As you graze upon the grass
You look like you are happy,
As you, as you, as you – graze,
I say 'Hello' to you.   *Kylie Elliott*

Blackie is a donkey from Spain,
Hit, push, kick, shove –
and not a lot of love.
That's what happened to him in Spain.

Blackie was brought here from Spain,
He is now in no pain.
We will see him in Sidmouth in Devon,
He thinks he is now in heaven,
Thank goodness he is not still in Spain.

Dawn Hart

(both at St Mary's School, Beaminster, Dorset)

171

1. Is it advisable to leave a NYLON headcollar on all the time?

    A. Yes
    B. No ✓
    C. Depends on the circumstances

2. On which side of the donkey should YOU be when you lead him?

    A. Left ✓
    B. Right
    C. Directly in front of him.

3. While leading the donkey should you be at his?

    A. Head
    B. Stomach
    C. Shoulder ✓

4. Which of the following would you NOT use for bedding your donkey?

    A. Straw
    B. Hay ✓
    C. Wood shavings

5. How often should you clean your donkey's stable out?

    A. At least once a month
    B. At least once a week
    C. At least once a day ✓

6. What do you use a metal curry comb for?

    A. To clean the donkey's coat
    B. To pick out the feet with
    C. To clean the body brush with ✓

7. How can you tell a donkey's age?

    A. By his general health
    B. By the use of his nose
    C. By his teeth ✓

8. Would you feed a donkey meat sandwiches?

    A. Yes, it's good for him
    B. No, it's very harmful to feed him meat ✓
    C. It makes no difference

9. What bulk foods form the main part of the donkey diet?

    A. Oats/pony cubes
    B. Cakes and sweets
    ✓*C. Hay, straw and/or grass*

10. Where do you find his withers?

    ✓*A. Top of the shoulder*
    B. Head
    C. Leg

(Answers on p. 176)

6–11 Years Old   Test Two   Practical

1. Approach a donkey and put a head collar on

2. Lead a donkey in hand

3. Tie up a donkey

4. Pick his feet out

5. Fill up a hay net

6. Explain how to worm a donkey

7. Clean a pair of stirrups and leathers

8. Put a pair of reins on a bridle

9. Check him over for injury

10. Turn a donkey out.

1. Which side is called the near side?

    ✓A. *The donkey's left*
    B. *The donkey's right*
    C. *The donkey's front*

2. Which side is it correct to mount and lead from?

    ✓A. *The donkey's left*
    B. *The donkey's right*
    C. *Either is correct*

3. How deep should a donkey's bed be?

    A. *At least 2 inches*
    ✓B. *At least 4 inches*
    C. *At least 6 inches*

4. How often should you muck out?

    ✓A. *Once a day*
    B. *Once every three days*
    C. *Once a week*

5. Which of the following is the odd one out?

    ✗A. *Hay*
    B. *Straw*
    ✓C. *Shavings*

6. How often should you worm a donkey?

    A. *Once a year*
    ✓B. *Every 6 – 8 months*
    C. *Every 9 months*

7. How does a donkey get worms?

    A. *They are born with them*
    B. *From an infection*
    ✓C. *Pick them up while grazing*

8. Where would you find a PASTERN?

    A. *On the muck heap*
    B. *On the donkey's head*
    ✓C. *On the donkey's leg*

9. Which of the following is poisonous to a donkey?

    A. Oats
    ✓*B. Yew*
    C. Grass

10. What is a metal curry comb for?

    ✓*A. To clean the body brushes*
    B. To groom the donkeys with
    C. To comb the mane and tail

(Answers on p. 176)

11–16 Years Old   Test Two   Practical

1. Groom a donkey

2. Muck out a stable

3. Put a bed down

4. Fill and tie up a hay net

5. Know the difference between hay and straw and good from bad in each

6. Describe basic feeding of a donkey

7. Tack a donkey up

8. Re-assemble a snaffle bridle

9. Clean a saddle

10. Put on a tail bandage

Sue Brennan

Answers to quizzes in Children's Section

Answers to crossword on p. 151

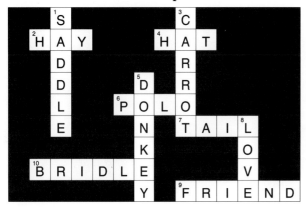

Answers to crossword on p. 156

Answer to quiz 'which word appears twice?' on p. 154: FOAL

Answer to Word Search on p. 155: hoof pick, water brush, hoof oil, curry comb, dandy brush, body brush, mane comb, wisp, sponge, stable rubber.

Answers to questions for young children on pp. 157-9

1. Halter
2. Straw
3. Water
4. Hay
5. Saddle
6. Horse box
7. Hay net
8. Fork
9. Hoof pick
10. Dandy brush
11. Stable

Answers to puzzle time on p. 162:

1. FIELD
2. STABLE
3. SHELTER
4. STRAW
5. BUCKET
6. HAY NET
7. HEAD COLLAR
8. LEADING REIN
9. BODY BRUSH
10. DANDY BRUSH
11. CURRY COMB
12. HOOF PICK
13. HOOF OIL
14. SADDLE
15. BRIDLE
16. REINS
17. STIRRUPS
18. GIRTH
19. CRUPPER
20. BLANKET

Answers to Quiz on pp. 168-9

1. A 2. B 3. A 4. C 5. B 6. C 7. B 8. B 9. C 10. D

Answers to 6-11 years old
test one written paper on pp. 172-3:

1. No
2. Left
3. Shoulder
4. Hay
5. At least once a day
6. To clean the body brush with
7. By his teeth
8. No, it is very harmful to feed him meat
9. Hay, straw and/or grass
10. Top of the shoulder

Answers to 11-16 years old
test one written paper on pp. 174-5:

1. The donkey's left
2. The donkey's left but either is correct (When on the road it is correct to lead from the right.)
3. At least 4 inches
4. Once a day
5. Wood shavings
6. Every 6-8 weeks
7. They pick them up while grazing
8. On the donkey's leg
9. Yew
10. To clean the body brushes